IO 27875

HUMAN RIGHTS IN CUBA: A SQUANDERED OPPORTUNITY

HEARING

BEFORE THE

SUBCOMMITTEE ON AFRICA, GLOBAL HEALTH, GLOBAL HUMAN RIGHTS, AND INTERNATIONAL ORGANIZATIONS

OF THE

COMMITTEE ON FOREIGN AFFAIRS HOUSE OF REPRESENTATIVES

ONE HUNDRED FOURTEENTH CONGRESS

FIRST SESSION

—————

FEBRUARY 5, 2015

—————

Serial No. 114–13

—————

Printed for the use of the Committee on Foreign Affairs

Available via the World Wide Web: http://www.foreignaffairs.house.gov/ or http://www.gpo.gov/fdsys/

—————

U.S. GOVERNMENT PUBLISHING OFFICE

93–159PDF   WASHINGTON : 2015

For sale by the Superintendent of Documents, U.S. Government Publishing Office
Internet: bookstore.gpo.gov   Phone: toll free (866) 512–1800; DC area (202) 512–1800
Fax: (202) 512–2104   Mail: Stop IDCC, Washington, DC 20402–0001

COMMITTEE ON FOREIGN AFFAIRS

EDWARD R. ROYCE, California, *Chairman*

CHRISTOPHER H. SMITH, New Jersey
ILEANA ROS-LEHTINEN, Florida
DANA ROHRABACHER, California
STEVE CHABOT, Ohio
JOE WILSON, South Carolina
MICHAEL T. McCAUL, Texas
TED POE, Texas
MATT SALMON, Arizona
DARRELL E. ISSA, California
TOM MARINO, Pennsylvania
JEFF DUNCAN, South Carolina
MO BROOKS, Alabama
PAUL COOK, California
RANDY K. WEBER SR., Texas
SCOTT PERRY, Pennsylvania
RON DeSANTIS, Florida
MARK MEADOWS, North Carolina
TED S. YOHO, Florida
CURT CLAWSON, Florida
SCOTT DesJARLAIS, Tennessee
REID J. RIBBLE, Wisconsin
DAVID A. TROTT, Michigan
LEE M. ZELDIN, New York
TOM EMMER, Minnesota

ELIOT L. ENGEL, New York
BRAD SHERMAN, California
GREGORY W. MEEKS, New York
ALBIO SIRES, New Jersey
GERALD E. CONNOLLY, Virginia
THEODORE E. DEUTCH, Florida
BRIAN HIGGINS, New York
KAREN BASS, California
WILLIAM KEATING, Massachusetts
DAVID CICILLINE, Rhode Island
ALAN GRAYSON, Florida
AMI BERA, California
ALAN S. LOWENTHAL, California
GRACE MENG, New York
LOIS FRANKEL, Florida
TULSI GABBARD, Hawaii
JOAQUIN CASTRO, Texas
ROBIN L. KELLY, Illinois
BRENDAN F. BOYLE, Pennsylvania

AMY PORTER, *Chief of Staff*　　THOMAS SHEEHY, *Staff Director*

JASON STEINBAUM, *Democratic Staff Director*

———

SUBCOMMITTEE ON AFRICA, GLOBAL HEALTH, GLOBAL HUMAN RIGHTS, AND INTERNATIONAL ORGANIZATIONS

CHRISTOPHER H. SMITH, New Jersey, *Chairman*

MARK MEADOWS, North Carolina
CURT CLAWSON, Florida
SCOTT DesJARLAIS, Tennessee
TOM EMMER, Minnesota

KAREN BASS, California
DAVID CICILLINE, Rhode Island
AMI BERA, California

CONTENTS

HUMAN RIGHTS IN CUBA:
A SQUANDERED OPPORTUNITY

THURSDAY, FEBRUARY 5, 2015

House of Representatives,
Subcommittee on Africa, Global Health,
Global Human Rights, and International Organizations,
Committee on Foreign Affairs,
Washington, DC.

The subcommittee met, pursuant to notice, at 10:03 a.m., in room 2172, Rayburn House Office Building, Hon. Christopher H. Smith (chairman of the subcommittee) presiding.

Mr. SMITH. Good morning to everyone. And welcome to this very timely and important hearing on human rights in Cuba.

We are here to examine the state of human rights, which is a very timely topic indeed, given the Obama administration's sea change in policy toward Cuba announced at the end of last year.

We are here to ask whether, in undertaking this change in policy, the Obama administration used the considerable leverage that it wields to seek to better the condition of the Cuban people or whether, as I fear, an opportunity that was squandered in its haste to achieve a diplomatic breakthrough and even create a legacy for the President.

Thus this hearing is not only about Castro regime accountability, but also the Obama administration's accountability, with Congress exercising its role of both oversight and as a bully pulpit for reminding the world that Cuba remains a Communist dictatorship which continues to arrest political dissidents—and I would underscore an estimated 178 political dissidents in the last month alone—and one whose caudillo, Raul Castro, has declared would not change, even in response to the Obama administration's concessions.

This Castro regime continues to harbor fugitives from justice, such as Joanne Chesimard, who was convicted in the 1973 murder of a state trooper in my own home State of New Jersey. Officer Werner Foerster was gunned down gangland style after she escaped from prison. Indeed, just yesterday we had the Assistant Secretary of State for the Western Hemisphere, Roberta Jacobson, appear before the Committee on Foreign Affairs. I asked her what the response of the Cuban Government was when she raised the issue of the return of Joanne Chesimard to justice. She replied that the Cuban Government stated that it was, "Not interested in discussing her return." That is absolutely unacceptable.

I have in my hands a statement, which I ask to be submitted for the record, from Christopher Burgos, the president of the State Troopers' Fraternal Association of New Jersey, wherein he states on behalf of our Jersey state troopers that, ''We are shocked and very disappointed that returning a convicted killer of a state trooper was not already demanded and accomplished in the context of the steps announced by the White House regarding this despotic dictatorship.''

I would also point out, as an aside, that both President Burgos and New Jersey State Police Superintendent Colonel Rick Fuentes both very much wanted to be here, and we will have another hearing to hear from them. And I look forward to that follow-up hearing.

But, fortunately, we do have with us and it is a tremendous honor and a privilege to have with us today three extraordinarily brave and uniquely qualified witnesses to the brutality of the Cuban dictatorship, three human rights activists who at great personal cost to themselves and their families have and continue to stand up for human dignity.

We will hear about the deplorable state of human rights in Cuba. Just read the State Department report on human rights as well as reporting that has been done by other NGOs and it couldn't be more clear that human rights are violated with impunity by the Castro brothers and their regime.

I would note parenthetically that years ago, during the Reagan administration, I met with Armando Valladares, who spent almost two decades in the Cuban gulag system. And I will never forget, when I read his book—he actually led the delegation from the United States to the U.N. Commission on Human Rights. As a matter of fact, Ileana and her staff—we went time and time again to that Commission, asking them to look at the deplorable state of human rights in Cuba.

When I was with Armando Valladares, I was in awe of his courage as well. He was able to get the U.N. to look at, pass a resolution condemning the deplorable situation in Cuba, and to deploy a team to go to the prisons and investigate these terrible abuses of human rights.

There were promises made by Fidel Castro that there would be no retaliation whatsoever against those who spoke in prison and the family members who came forward and friends to bear witness to a terrible set of truths.

Everybody was retaliated against, the people in the prisons as well as their families. And, regrettably, the U.N. was unable—perhaps unwilling, but certainly unable, to do anything to mitigate or to stop that retaliation.

I have pushed for years to go to Cuba. I have been denied a visa for two decades or so. I want to go to the prisons. Of course, I will meet with Fidel if I am able to lead a delegation or even go on my own with my staff. We can't get that visa. Both Frank Wolf and I tried a number of times, and it got so bad that, at one point, Fidel Castro said that we were provocateurs. I want to go meet with the dissidents.

Frank Wolf and I got into prisons in the Soviet Union, the infamous Perm Camp 35, where people like Natan Sharansky suffered and were tortured by that Communist dictatorship. When Xanana Gusmão, who became the President of East Timor—I went and saw him when he was in Jakarta and went to prisons all over the world, but we can't get into Cuba. We even got into Beijing Prison Number 2, where 40 Tiananmen Square activists were being forced to do gulag labor, heads shaved, gone, they looked like concentration camp victims.

And, yet, Mr. Wolf and I could not and I cannot get into those prisons. So I will be asking the government again—I have already asked, and I have asked our Government to help facilitate it—to go to the prisons.

And even on the ICRC, yesterday the Red Cross—I asked Secretary Jacobson—I said, ''You know, much has been made that the ICRC might be able to get into the country.'' That is unacceptable. Get into the prisons. And, again, there needs—there has to be absolutely no retaliation to those who speak out.

I would point out that, after testifying here today in public—and I thank C–SPAN especially and the journalists for taking this story and making Americans aware of what is actually happening in Cuba. Right now, as we meet, they will be returning to Cuba—and this committee and I know the entire Congress will be watching—to ensure that their safety and well-being and health is not further jeopardized.

But the courage to come forward to congressional hearings—our friends over on the Senate side received compelling testimony as well—and to bear witness to an ugly truth of torture—I would ask everyone to go back and reread ''Against All Hope,'' Armando Valladares' famous book. He talked about tortures that I don't even want to mention in public, they are so despicable, of putting dissidents in vats of excrement so bad that it went into their ears and nose and they got infections.

Armando Valladares told me that, when he and his wife—when they finally got to the United States and got asylum—that he couldn't even change his children's diapers because the smell of excrement brought back instantaneously, like, PTSD, remembrances of that kind of degrading cruelty imposed upon them.

The Castro brothers and many in this regime ought to be at The Hague for crimes against humanity. That is how bad it is. These are among the worst abuses of human rights in the entire world.

So, again, I want to welcome our brave and courageous witnesses.

I want to thank Ileana Ros-Lehtinen and Mario Diaz-Balart. Ileana has been such a leader for so long in raising the truth of what is going on in this gulag island.

I have much more to say, but I will put the rest of it into the record.

But I do want to thank our witnesses again, and I look forward to hearing their testimony.

[The prepared statement of Mr. Smith follows:]

CHRISTOPHER H. SMITH
4TH DISTRICT, NEW JERSEY

CONSTITUENT SERVICE CENTERS:

MONMOUTH
112 Village Center Drive
Freehold, NJ 07728-2510
(732) 780-3035

OCEAN
405 Route 539
Plumsted, NJ 08514-2903
(609) 286-2571; (732) 350-2300

MERCER
4573 South Broad Street
Hamilton, NJ 08620-2215
(609) 585-7878

2373 Rayburn House Office Building
Washington, DC 20515-3004
(202) 225-3765

Congress of the United States
House of Representatives

SENIOR MEMBER, FOREIGN AFFAIRS
COMMITTEE

CHAIRMAN, AFRICA, GLOBAL HEALTH,
GLOBAL HUMAN RIGHTS, AND
INTERNATIONAL ORGANIZATIONS
SUBCOMMITTEE

WESTERN HEMISPHERE
SUBCOMMITTEE

CO-CHAIRMAN, COMMISSION ON SECURITY
AND COOPERATION IN EUROPE

CO-CHAIRMAN, CONGRESSIONAL-EXECUTIVE
COMMISSION ON CHINA

DEAN, NEW JERSEY DELEGATION

http://chrissmith.house.gov

"Human Rights in Cuba: A Squandered Opportunity"

Remarks by Chairman Chris Smith (NJ-04)
House Subcommittee on Africa, Global Health,
Global Human Rights and Int'l Organizations
February 5, 2015

Good morning. We are here today to examine the state of human rights in Cuba, which is a very timely topic indeed, given the Obama Administration's sea change in policy toward Cuba announced at the end of last year.

We are here to ask whether in undertaking this change in policy, the Obama Administration used the considerable leverage that it wields to seek to better the condition of the Cuban people, or whether, as I fear, an opportunity was squandered in its haste to achieve a diplomatic breakthrough and create a legacy for the President.

Thus this hearing is not only about Castro regime accountability, but also Obama Administration accountability, with Congress exercising its role of both oversight and as a bully pulpit for reminding the world that Cuba remains a Communist dictatorship which continues to arrest political dissidents – an estimated 178 in this last month alone – and one whose *caudillo*, Raul Castro, has declared would not change, even in response to the Obama Administrations concessions.

This Castro regime continues to harbor fugitives from justice such as Joanne Chesimard, who was convicted in the 1973 murder of a state trooper in my home state of New Jersey, Officer Werner Foerster. Indeed, just yesterday, we had the Assistant Secretary of State for the Western Hemisphere Roberta Jacobson appear before the full Foreign Affairs Committee. I asked her what the response of the Cuban government was when she raised the issue of the return of Joanne Chesimard to justice. She replied that the Cuban government stated that it was "not interested in discussing her return."

This is unacceptable. I have here in my hands a statement which I ask to be submitted for the record from Christopher J. Burgos, the President of the State Troopers Fraternal Organization of New Jersey, wherein he states on behalf of our Jersey State Troopers that "We are shocked and very disappointed that returning a convicted killer of a State Trooper was not already demanded and accomplished in the context of the steps announced by the White House regarding this despotic dictatorship."

-Chairman of the following member organizations: Task Force on Alzheimer's Disease • Bi-Partisan Coalition for Combating Anti-Semitism • Lyme Disease Caucus
Coalition for Autism Research and Education • Global Internet Freedom Caucus • Bi-Partisan Congressional Pro-Life Caucus • Bosnia Caucus • Poland Caucus
Ad Hoc Congressional Committee for Irish Affairs • Congressional Caucus on Human Trafficking • Vietnam Caucus • Congressional Heart and Stroke Coalition

I also would like to point out as an aside that both President Burgos and New Jersey State Police Superintendent Colonel Rick Fuentes both very much had wanted to be here today to present testimony in person, and I look forward to having them here for a follow up hearing on this topic which is very important to the people of my State.

But fortunately, we do have with us three very brave and uniquely qualified witnesses to the brutality of the Cuban dictatorship, three human rights activists who at great personal cost to themselves and their families stood up for human dignity.

We will hear about the deplorable state of human rights in Cuba, how Afro-Cubans in particular face discrimination on a day-to-day basis, and the brutality with which human rights activists, including women, are treated. We will hear of murders sanctioned by the government, of beatings, of arrests and re-arrests.

And I would also like to point out that after testifying here, in public, two of our witnesses will be returning to Cuba. They know that while they may not be arrested upon their return, one day the regime will exact a price against them for their temerity. Yet they insist on appearing here, so that they can share the truth of what is happening in their beloved isle. What bravery!

I therefore would like to dedicate this hearing to the Cuban people, who have suffered for so many decades under the brutal regime of the Castro brothers, and to thank our witnesses for testifying. I also would like to thank in particular my dear friend and colleague, Ileana Ros-Lehtinen, for her leadership day-in-and-day-out, in good weather and in bad, on behalf of the people of not only Cuba, but in countries such as Venezuela, China and Viet Nam, where the people continue to suffer under oppressive rulers. Thank you, Ileana, for your leadership and moral clarity.

It is thus my belief that there should be no easing of the pressure until Cuba has met definitive and concrete human rights and democratic milestones. Among thee milestones are the release of *all* political prisoners, the end of harassment and a policy of releasing and then re-jailing, the ending of restrictions on freedom of speech and the press, and on the rights of Assembly. Moreover, the Church must be allowed to conduct its affairs fully and freely without government interference.

And, finally, the Castro regime must be held to account for their harboring of some seventy fugitives from justice, including Joanne Chesimard, who is on the FBI's Most Wanted Terrorist list.

To that end, I would like to state that I intend to introduce legislation that will complement our existing legislation on Cuba, in particular Helms-Burton, making sure that important human rights milestones are met before our government makes concessions that are effectively unilateral, squandering leverage. I would like to invite my colleagues to consider joining as co-sponsors.

With that, thank you.

_____

Mr. SMITH. And I yield to my good friend and colleague, Ms. Bass, the gentlelady from California.

Mr. CICILLINE. Mr. Chairman, if——

Mr. SMITH. Sure.

Mr. CICILLINE. Mr. Chairman, I would ask unanimous consent to address the committee for about a minute or so.

Mr. Chairman, I just want to take a brief moment before we turn to the very serious topic of human rights in Cuba to respond to a statement from this subcommittee's last hearing that had troubling interpretations.

While discussing your position on marriage equality, you made comments and engaged in a line of questioning that some understood as suggesting that lesbian, gay, bisexual, and transgender people do not have basic human rights.

After exchanging letters with you, I think it is important to note that, while we do have very different opinions on marriage equality—you strongly oppose it; I strongly support it—we both agree that, unequivocally, LGBT people have the same rights as all other people to live lives free from violence and persecution.

In your letter and your public statement, you said that you—and I quote—"unequivocally oppose acts of violence against anyone and believe that human rights apply to all" and that—and I quote again—"all individuals, including LGBT persons, should be treated with respect and compassion."

I want to thank you for the opportunity to clear up the confusion over your statement and to reaffirm our shared passion for protecting the human rights of all people. The policy of the United States is absolutely clear. LGBT rights are human rights, and LGBT people are entitled to live lives free from violence, intimidation, discrimination, and harm.

And I thank you, Mr. Chairman. And I yield back.

Mr. SMITH. Okay. Thank you, Mr. Cicilline.

I would just again say we do have a fundamental difference. I don't support homosexual marriage. I know you do, and I certainly respect your views.

And I do want to point out that I am for universally recognized human rights for all. And there is no treaty that recognizes a right to marriage for homosexuals. But, again, I am glad we were able to work together.

Okay. Why don't you go. Okay. Go ahead.

Ms. BASS. Okay. Thank you, Mr. Chair.

And I do appreciate the clarification of that because I know, with your long record on human rights, that you would never be okay with the egregious human rights violations that are taking place around the world in the LGBT community and that there is a fundamental difference between marriage, which many people have a difference around, but I know that there is no difference around LGBT rights and the violence and opposing the violence against LGBT people. So thank you for that.

Today's hearing on human rights in Cuba is in the context of President Obama's recent announcement. I said yesterday in our Foreign Affairs Committee that sometimes, in talking about Cuba, it is difficult because two of my colleagues that are on the other side of the aisle right now in this hearing have family history and personal situations that make it very difficult if one does have a difference of opinion. I want to, one, respect and acknowledge what my colleagues have been through and what their families have been through and, with no disrespect or disregard for those histories, want to take a few minutes and propose a different viewpoint.

You know, the President's policy of opening up relations with Cuba I actually think is a very good thing, especially for people who are concerned about human rights.

During the five decades that we have not had relations with the Cuban Government and the Cuban people, the Cuban economy did experience multiple economic shocks which really produced hardships for the people, but none of it really produced the kind of popular uprisings or internal resistance that might have led to a change in government.

I also think that the embargo prohibited diplomatic and economic engagement between the U.S. and Cuba. And I think that that many times is the ways in which societies become more open and accountable and democratic and trade and cultural exchange becomes mutually beneficial.

I think the embargo has impeded U.S. relations throughout the Western Hemisphere, as many Latin American nations viewed the embargo itself as a human rights violation against the Cuban people.

I have to say that, as a U.S. citizen, I definitely consider it my human right to be able to travel to any nation on the Earth, and I have resented the fact that it has been difficult—Americans can go to Cuba, and I have been to Cuba, but it is very, very difficult to go there.

And I don't believe—and I might be wrong—but I don't believe that we have that restriction against any other nation in the world, including Iran, North Korea, and Saudi Arabia, all of which have extremely troubling human rights records.

Such travel restrictions, as well as those of trade, also violate the freedom of U.S. citizens, and recent polling by CBS, ABC News and the Washington Post revealed that a majority of Americans are supportive of moving away from the policy of disengagement and toward reestablishing ties with Cuba.

I also think that engagement would be good for the Cuban people, as people-to-people exchanges and the Cuban-American family travel would increase cultural engagement, assist in family reunification. And this opening of space will provide improved access to Cuba for nongovernmental organizations that are focused on governance and human rights as well as facilitating technical assistance to Cuban civil society groups concerned with improved standards of economic and personal freedoms.

I do have to say—Mr. Chair, you mentioned about visiting prisons in Cuba. When I did go, I did visit Alan Gross and I visited him in prison. And I think that it was important that, during the time that Mr. Gross was incarcerated, that a number of Members of Congress went over and visited him and pushed for his release, and I think that that was a contributing factor.

Again, I just feel that you really can't change people and governments whom you refuse to engage with. And so increased engagement, to me, seems like it would be a contributing factor to improving the human rights situation on the island of Cuba.

And I look forward to the testimony from our witnesses today. Thank you.

Mr. SMITH. Thank you, Karen.

I would like to now yield to the chairwoman emeritus of the Committee on Foreign Affairs, Congresswoman Ileana Ros-Lehtinen.

Ms. ROS-LEHTINEN. Thank you very much.

And I also am glad that Mr. Gross is home. But if by visiting Mr. Gross you believe that you have been to a Cuban jail, maybe these dissidents here could tell you what a Cuban jail is really like. But we are thankful that he is home. Or we could ask someone like Mr. Basilio Guzman, who is in the audience today, he served 22 years in Castro's prison.

And, Mr. Smith, I would like to request unanimous consent to submit into the record a letter from the International Committee of Former Cuban Political Prisoners based in Union City, New Jersey, documenting a list of the many Cubans who are still languishing in Castro's gulag.

And thank you to Mr. Guzman for pointing that out.

Mr. SMITH. Without objection, so ordered.

Ms. ROS-LEHTINEN. Thank you.

Mr. Smith, I want to thank you so very much for convening this important hearing for your unyielding and passionate commitment to human rights, to freedom, not just for the oppressed people of Cuba, but for all people everywhere who suffer under oppressive regimes and who continue to seek the most basic and fundamental rights for many people that they take for granted. Everywhere there is an oppressed person, a political prisoner, there you will find Mr. Smith. So we thank you for that.

I also want to welcome our wonderful witnesses: Berta Soler, Sara Fonseca, and Antunez, all champions of freedom on the island and the face of what the democratic future of Cuba will look like—look at those faces—that is the Cuba now. That is the free Cuba of tomorrow.

These are brave pro-democracy activists who have seen firsthand the brutality of the regime by the constant arrests and beatings that they have had to endure, the isolation that they have had to endure while in jail, they did not have food prepared especially for them. They were starved. And after this hearing, they will be going back to Cuba, amazingly enough, as you pointed out, Mr. Smith, to continue the fight for freedom and democracy.

Berta, as a matter of fact, she will be marching with her sisters, the Ladies in White—Las Damas de Blanco—this very Sunday. And, by the way, while all these negotiations are going on, there were 13 detentions of the Ladies in White just last Sunday. So if you think everything is rosy and bright and terrific and all wonderful, just ask these three dissidents what life is like for them. Very unlike what we hear from others.

Our witnesses are just three of the countless faces of Cuba who represent the future, who the administration has shut out of the negotiations. And rarely are they invited to meet with visiting dignitaries. We are glad that they get the chance to go to Cuba. Rarely do they invite dissidents who disagree with this administration.

These are the people who have to suffer the consequences of the administration's decisions. It is easy for the President to change this policy in his ivory tower. These are the faces who must now suffer under a Castro regime reenergized by President Obama's policies, by its injections of cash.

The President's December 17th announcement serves to embolden the regime by implying that it can continue its repressive machinery with impunity. Raul Castro said, ''We will not change,'' and we look the other way. It undercuts and it demoralizes the brave freedom fighters in Cuba who rightfully believe that the U.S. has turned its back on them. But don't confuse the U.S. people with the administration, just like we don't confuse the Castro regime with the people of Cuba.

And for what are these negotiations? So that more Americans can travel to Cuba and see what the regime wants them to see, all the while the regime fills its coffers and we ignore the truth. Because who owns the hotels? The Castro regime. Who runs the hotels? The Castro military. The truth about the Cuban regime is that it is a regime that severely punishes dissidents even to this day.

El Dkano was sentenced to 1 year in prison just last week, a young rapper. A rapper is a threat to this regime. Did he committee a crime? No. His charge was dangerousness which could lead to a crime. It is the precogs of that movie. They predict that you are going to commit a crime; so, they arrest you before you commit it. This regime forbids reform and will do anything to maintain its grip on power.

The censorship apparatus, one of the most comprehensive in the world. It forbids Cubans from listening to independent, private, or foreign broadcasts and even censors the signal of its own allies' televised propaganda.

It is important, Mr. Chairman, that we understand exactly the kind of murderous regime we are dealing with in Cuba and that President Obama wants to normalize relations with.

On November 4, 1999, the House Committee on International Relations convened a congressional hearing entitled, ''The Cuban Program: Torture of American Prisoners By Cuban Agents.'' At that hearing, you remember, Mr. Chairman, we heard testimony from American POWs—prisoners of war—who were tortured at a prison camp in North Vietnam known as the ''Zoo'' during the period of August 1967 to August 1968. According to reports, 19 of those courageous servicemen were psychologically tortured and beaten by Cuban agents working under orders from Hanoi.

And while the State Department led the negotiations last month in Havana, its very own Country Reports on Human Rights for 2013 states this: ''The following additional abuses continued: Harsh prison conditions, arbitrary arrests, selective prosecution, denial of free trial''—this is from the State Department, our State Department; they are still negotiating with Castro while this is going on—''authorities interfered with privacy, engaging in pervasive monitoring of private conversations. The government did not respect freedom of speech and press, severely restricted Internet access and maintained a monopoly on media outlets, circumscribed academic freedom, and maintained significant restrictions on the ability of religious groups to meet and worship''—our own State Department—''The government refused to recognize independent human rights groups or permit them to function legally.'' They can tell you about that. ''In addition, the government continued to prevent workers from forming independent unions.'' Where are these voices who are so much for independent unions here in the United States? ''But not for you. You are not good enough. I'm sorry. No union for you.''

''Human rights abuses were official acts committed at the direction of the government.'' Our own State Department says this. ''Impunity for the perpetrators remained widespread.'' Because I could continue.

Mr. Chairman, we cannot be The Land of the Free across the world if this administration doesn't defend democracy right here in our own hemisphere. We cannot call for democratic reform and values throughout the world if we abandon them 90 miles from our shores.

Thank you, Mr. Chairman, for this time.

Welcome to our panelists.

Mr. SMITH. Chairwoman Ros-Lehtinen, thank you for that extraordinarily powerful statement and for your consistent support, again, not only of the Cuban people, but people who are dealing with tyrannies all over the world.

Ms. ROS-LEHTINEN. I hope you get your visa.

Mr. SMITH. Thank you.

Ms. ROS-LEHTINEN. Don't hold your breath.

Mr. SMITH. I would like to now yield to my friend and colleague, Mr. Cicilline.

Mr. CICILLINE. Thank you, Mr. Chairman. And I want to thank you and Ranking Member Bass for calling today's hearing on this very important issue.

I particularly want to thank the witnesses who are here today and thank you in advance for sharing your insight and your experiences. And I know that some of you are bravely joining us today to share very personal stories of very difficult and painful experiences, and we are really indebted to you for your willingness to do that.

As I discussed yesterday with the administration witnesses during our full committee hearing, I, like many, continue to have deep concerns about how the Cuban Government treats its citizens. But it is clear that the United States policy on Cuba over the past several decades has not worked either.

And I am hopeful that President Obama's effort to engage in real, substantive negotiations toward a more honest cultural exchange, economic trade, and diplomatic ties with Cuba will ultimately benefit the United States and, more importantly, the Cuban people.

I hope the Cuban Government will come to the negotiating table with a real desire to work with the United States toward a more free, open, and tolerant society for the Cuban people. And it is very important for us to pay close attention to the ongoing negotiations to make sure that any changes are implemented in a way that maintains our commitment to promoting basic values and human rights.

So I thank the witnesses again for being here and look forward to your perspective as the relationship between the United States and Cuba begins to change.

And, with that, I yield back, Mr. Chairman.

Mr. SMITH. Thank you, Mr. Cicilline.

Now I yield to my good friend and colleague who has been a very powerful voice, Mario Diaz-Balart, and thank him for joining us. He is a member of the Appropriations Committee, and he does us the honor of being here today.

Mr. DIAZ-BALART. Mr. Chairman, let me first thank you for the opportunity to sit in for a few minutes. I will not be able to stay for the entirety of the hearing because I do have other meetings to go to.

But I could not let this moment pass without first thanking you, sir, for your just steadfast leadership and your consistent leadership, whether it has been fighting for freedom and supporting the opposition in Vietnam and Communist China and North Korea. Wherever there has been oppression, Mr. Chairman, you have always been consistent, just like Chairwoman Emeritus Ileana Ros-Lehtinen. I want to thank both of you.

And I just want to make a couple of comments. And the ranking member, who was very kind in her introduction, mentioned about how some of us might have some family history. The issue of human rights has nothing to do with family history. Because I, for one, am opposed to oppression in Communist China, in North Korea, in Vietnam.

And I don't know. I was a very young man when we had sanctions against South Africa, and I supported the sanctions in South Africa. I am assuming that the ranking member was also opposed to sanctions in South Africa because I am assuming, obviously, that she is also as consistent as the chairman is on these issues.

I supported as a young man those sanctions against South Africa because doing business with the apartheid regime was not helping the folks who were struggling for freedom in South Africa. All it did was help prop up that regime in South Africa.

So, Mr. Chairman, I couldn't let this time slide by without being here.

Ms. BASS. May I ask the gentlemen to yield for a second?

Mr. DIAZ-BALART. Of course. With all pleasure.

Ms. BASS. You know, I really was only trying to acknowledge the fact that I realize people had personal situations.

Mr. DIAZ-BALART. And I appreciate that.

Ms. BASS. I wasn't trying to say that, you know, that is the only reason you are concerned about Cuba. It is just hard if you have a different opinion. I just wanted to respect what I knew you and Ileana's family had been through. That was all.

Mr. DIAZ-BALART. And I thank the ranking woman, as I said, for your kind statements. I took it as a kind statement. So I want to make sure of that. But I am just saying that the issue of human rights and the consistency on that is important.

When we look at the folks that are here today—I mentioned South Africa—in front of us today are the Mandelas, are the Havels, are the future leaders of the free and democratic Cuba.

When folks talk about Cuba, they sometimes confuse the regime with Cuba. No. This is Cuba in front of us today, they who have spent years in prison. Jorge Luis Garcia Perez, Antunez, 17 years in prison. By the way, ask him about the conditions of the prisons.

Ask Iris Aguilera about how well the Cuban people are treated. Ask Sara Marta Fonseca. Just go to YouTube and look at her videos to find out how respected and how well the Cuban people who dare just speak out for freedom are treated.

Ask Berta Soler about what happens when you just walk peacefully with a flower in your hand going to church and asking for freedom of their relatives. Ask her how the Cuban people are treated.

So at a time when during the State of the Union our President spoke about Cuba—and, by the way, for the first time in my recollection did I see a President speak in the State of the Union about Cuba and not even mention, not even mention, human rights, not even mention democracy, not even mention, not even give lip service, to elections in Cuba.

I am grateful to you, Mr. Chairman, for bringing these heros, the future leaders, them and others—the future leaders of Cuba, to this, the United States Congress, to testify.

Because, again, at a time when our President has decided to ignore the repression, the arrests, heck, even the sending of arms to North Korea from the Castro regime, this House, as it always has, will continue to stand with you, with the future leaders of Cuba, with the people of Cuba, and not with the regime.

I am grateful for the opportunity, Mr. Chairman, to be able to sit in here for a few minutes. Thank you, sir. I yield back.

Mr. SMITH. Mr. Diaz-Balart, thank you so very much for your very powerful statement, which has been consistent throughout the world.

I would like to now recognize Mr. Emmer, the gentleman from Minnesota.

Mr. EMMER. Well, thank you, Mr. Chair.

And it is difficult to follow that from a new colleague. So I won't. I won't try to follow that. All I will do is say thank you for this hearing, Mr. Chairman, especially in light of the President's decision to somehow restart diplomacy with the regime currently in charge in Cuba.

And there are still concerns for some of us about why the President would have used the process he used, side-stepping the State Department, having over a year of secret meetings that didn't involve normal process.

But that part aside, it really is all about the human rights and the Cuban people, which is why it is so interesting to me. The discussion about normalization of the relationship is really what we are here about today.

And I appreciate that you and the ranking member have decided that we are going to bring in some people to talk about some basic freedoms, the situation, exercise the oversight that is the jurisdiction of this committee. Because, thankfully, the President has acknowledged that he does not have the authority to dismantle, as he suggested, the embargo and start to normalize relationships with Cuba. That is up to Congress. And, hopefully, it starts here today.

And we can talk about how people can have basic and fundamental rights to assemble with people that they want, to speak freely on their own behalf and, God forbid, even against their government and that people can actually practice their faith in public and be proud of it.

I am looking forward at being part of the process, and I thank you again for holding this hearing.

And for the witnesses, I look forward to your testimony today.

And I yield back.

Mr. SMITH. Thank you very much, Mr. Emmer.

I would like to yield to Mr. Pittenger.

Mr. PITTENGER. Thank you, Mr. Chairman.

Mr. SMITH. A leader on religious freedom especially in this Congress and on Chinese human rights.

Mr. PITTENGER. Well, thank you, Mr. Chairman. I deeply appreciate being here. And forgive me for being late. But I want to come to pay tremendous respect to those who have come to testify today.

Each of us are still searching on the merits of why the President would make the unilateral decision that he made to provide a diplomatic relationship with Cuba against the wisdom of a dozen previous Presidents.

What he has done is elevate a terrorist state. Along with Cuba is Syria, Sudan, Iran that are terrorist states. And now he has declared to the world that this state is acceptable to the United States. It is a very sad day.

I have worked for the last 30 years with missionaries in Cuba. They tell me the plight of the religious inequities and the challenges that they face in people trying to live out their faith.

So I am deeply concerned over the impact of what will happen, the elevation we have given to the Marxist doctrine that will be encouraged throughout the world. We have dealt with Cuba on an ongoing basis in the United Nations. They have sought to engage those who oppose the United States and our closest allies, including Israel.

So I am here to pay respect to you and thank you for your commitment and to clearly say to you that we stand with you, fully engaged, on behalf of the wonderful people of Cuba.

Thank you and God bless you.

Mr. SMITH. Thank you very much, Mr. Pittenger.

It is now a very distinct honor and privilege to welcome our very distinguished witnesses. They are doing here today in Washington that which they would not be able to do in Cuba, especially before that rogue congress where there is really no real election, there are no free and fair elections.

Let me begin first with Mr. Jorge Luis Garcia Perez, Antunez, who is a leader in the Cuban democratic movement. He was inspired early in life by reading the Universal Declaration of Human Rights, rejecting the Communist indoctrination that he was receiving in Cuba's schools.

Antunez, as he is known to us all as, is a leader of a nonviolent movement to promote human rights and democracy. He was arrested in 1990 for peacefully protesting the Castro brothers' oppressive regime and spent the next 17 years, 17 years, in jail as a political prisoner. He endured horrific torture, beatings, solitary confinement, and denial of needed medical care that almost cost him his life.

Since his release in 2007, Antunez has continued to advance the cause of freedom and human rights in Cuba. He also knows firsthand the discrimination suffered by Afro-Cubans on a daily basis, an underfocused-upon, aggressive racism employed by the Castro regime.

We will then hear from Ms. Berta Soler, who has been the leader of the Ladies in White movement following the death of the group's founder, Laura Pollan, in 2011. The Ladies in White is a movement of wives and female relatives of Cuban political prisoners, but now has evolved into a potent, powerful human rights group open to all Cuban women.

Ms. Soler and four other members of the Ladies in White received the Sakharov Prize for Freedom of Thought by European Parliament in 2006, but the Castro brothers barred them from attending the award ceremony.

She and her husband have remained in Cuba since his release, rejecting, rejecting, an offer of immigration from Spain in order to continue their struggle for human rights and democracy in Cuba.

I would also note that the Ladies in White have been nominated by Ileana Ros-Lehtinen and I and others in a joint request to the Nobel Peace Prize committee, along with Dr. Biscet, another Afro-Cuban and medical doctor who has been tortured horrifically as well.

He testified here, as you know, by way of a phone hookup and told us, Do not, do not, end the embargo. Get the conditions first. Get human rights and durable human rights at that before that embargo is lifted. And he said it even though there is great risk to himself in articulating that.

He pointed out, as many others have pointed out, that the Europeans have been trading with Cuba for decades with no amelioration whatsoever and have been a lifeline, frankly, to a dictatorship which Russia first provided, then Venezuela, and, unfortunately, trade coming from Europe and Canada.

Then we will hear from Ms. Sara Fonseca, who grew up in a household that opposed the Communist system based on their principles and their deep religious beliefs. Due to her family's faith, she was denied the right to complete her studies.

In 2004, she became a member of the Pro-Human Rights Party affiliated with the Andrei Sakharov Foundation. In 2009, she joined the Rosa Parks Civil Rights Women's Movement, for which she became the delegate in the city of Havana. That same year, she also began participating with the Ladies in White as a lady of support.

She and her family have experienced numerous state-organized mob attacks, and her house has been vandalized and searched by government agents dressed in civilian clothes. As a result, she has sought refugee status in the United States.

Then we will hear from Mr. Geoff Thale, who oversees the entire range of the Washington Office on Latin America's research and advocacy in Latin America policy and human rights issues. Along with a focus on specific countries and themes, Mr. Thale led the team that authored, ''Forging New Ties,'' WOLA's recommendations for new directions in U.S. policy toward Latin America.

Mr. Thale has studied Cuba issues since the mid-1990s and traveled to Cuba more than a dozen times—wish I could get that visa—including organizing delegations of academics and Members of Congress. He coordinates WOLA's advocacy of this issue with a coalition of business, agricultural, and human rights groups who favor lifting the general travel ban on Cuba.

I would like to now yield the floor to Antunez.

STATEMENT OF MR. JORGE LUIS GARCÍA PÉREZ, SECRETARY GENERAL, CUBAN NATIONAL CIVIC RESISTANCE FRONT

[The following statement and answers were delivered through an interpreter.]

Mr. GARCIA. Honorable Congressman Christopher Smith, good morning to all participating members.

My name is Jorge Luis Garcia Perez, Antunez. I am a former political prisoner who spent 17 continuous years of political imprisonment for the sole supposed crime of calling out in a public square in my hometown of Placetas for the implementation of reforms such as those that were taking place back then in Communist Europe.

Within the prisons, I remained steadfast in my condition as a political prisoner. And due to my constant struggle to denounce human rights violations from within prison walls, I was subjected to the most refined forms of torture and cruel punishment.

For example, on the morning of 14 October 1994, high ranking officers from the political police, in spite of the fact that my hands were handcuffed behind my back, sicced dogs on me. Because I did not accept the regime's indoctrination program within prison walls, I was sent to the most inhospitable and rigorous prisons.

Later, together with very courageous brothers from the prison, we founded the Pedro Luis Boitel Political Prisons Organization, which, in spite of repression, managed to unify hundreds of political prisoners in order to carry out civic resistance within the prison walls.

After I was released in 2007, I have continued with the struggle inside Cuba where I think it is most important. I am currently active in the Orlando Zapata Tamayo National Civic Resistance Front. This is a national organization which carries out protests in the defense of human rights throughout Cuba.

Today I am here in the name of my brothers and sisters of the resistance and most especially in the name of those who are imprisoned for their ideas, which there are dozens of. They have remained in prison in spite of the unconvincing process of release agreed upon by President Barack Obama and dictator Raul Castro.

Among my imprisoned brothers, I want to mention Ciro Alexis Casanova Perez, Ernesto Borjes Perez, Armando Sosa Fortuny, among others. These men are part of a long list of heros whose only crime has been, first of all, to oppose the dictatorship and, second of all, to continue resisting within prison walls.

A few days ago we learned that the President of this great and hospitable Nation had agreed with dictator Raul Castro to reestablish diplomatic relations as well as steps leading to the elimination of the embargo. And as if this were not enough, three confessed spies who participated in the murder of four U.S. citizens were exchanged for innocent contractor Alan Gross.

These agreements, which are considered by an important part of the Cuban resistance as a betrayal of the hopes for freedom of the Cuban people, are unacceptable because the principles and the freedom of a country do not belong to any government, no matter how powerful or influential this government may be.

There is underway an international effort expressed by the Obama-Castro accords to promote a supposed evolution within the Castro regime. This is a fraudulent change promoted by Castro regime in order to perpetuate itself in power.

This illusion is manipulated by the dictatorship in order to perpetuate itself in power. The Castro dictatorship cannot be reformed. The Castro dictatorship is based on the negation of democratic society and everything this represents. The Castro dictatorship not only seeks to control the Cuban people, it also seeks to export this repression. It seeks to export this repression to other countries such as Venezuela.

What does real change in Cuba mean? It means the restitution of all civil rights. It means the general amnesty for all political prisoners. It means the right to organize political parties and independent labor unions.

Real change in Cuba means free, real elections, internationally supervised free elections. It means the separation from power of the Castro brothers. This is recognized in current U.S. law toward Cuba, and it should remain so because it constitutes the best possible support for the Cuban resistance.

A majority of the Cuban resistance has signed onto the agreement for democracy in Cuba. This is a road map of 10 elemental points toward democracy in Cuba. We ask recognition from the Congress of the United States for this document and for what it represents as a clear path toward democracy in Cuba. I ask the American people and its freely elected Congress that it maintains its firm support for the right of the Cuban people to be free.

We may be close to true change in Cuba. The drop in the international price of oil, the instability of the Maduro regime in Venezuela which has been the main support of the Castro regime, the civic resistance which is widespread throughout the island, and how this resistance is increasingly coordinating itself, as is taking place with the forum for freedoms and rights, all indicate this.

This is the moment to demand real concessions from the Castro regime. Only this can mean normal relations between the United States and Cuba. Cubans can be as successful on the island as they have been abroad. What we need is freedom. The Cuban resistance struggles for this freedom. We need your understanding and your support.

Thank you.

[The prepared statement of Mr. Garcia follows:]

TESTIMONY OF JORGE LUIS GARCIA PEREZ "ANTUNEZ," BEFORE THE SUB COMMITTEE ON AFRICA, GLOBAL HEALTH, GLOBAL HUMAN RIGHTS, AND INTERNATIONAL ORGANIZATIONS OF THE COMMITTEE ON FOREIGN AFFAIRS OF THE HOUSE OF REPRESENTATIVES OF THE CONGRESS OF THE UNITED STATES

This testimony is being delivered in English by Orlando Gutierrez-Boronat

2 FEBRUARY 2015

My name is Jorge Luis Garcia Perez "Antunez." I am a former Cuban political prisoner, who served a sentence of 17 continuous years of imprisonment for calling out for political and economic reforms of the type then being carried out in Eastern Europe, in a public plaza in my home town of Placetas, in central Cuba.

I was subjected to torture and to cruel and unusual punishment during my time spent in prison for both calling out for reform, and for being a "plantado," a political prisoner who refuses to participate in Regime indoctrination programs. As a prisoner, I constantly denounced the human rights violations that we were subjected to. I was sent to the most inhospitable and distant prisons in my country. With fellow political prisoners, in 1995 we founded the Pedro Luis Boitel Political Prisoners Organization, which managed to organize hundreds of political prisoners throughout the island in an unprecedented fashion.

After my release in 2007, I have continued with the struggle for freedom from inside Cuba, where I think that it is most important. I am currently active in the Orlando Zapata Cuban National Civic Resistance Front, a combative coalition of regional pro-democracy organizations which carries out public protests in demand of respect for human rights throughout the island of Cuba.

For this activity, and for having decided not to abandon my country, but instead to remain there, in order to continue with the struggle, my family and I have been subjected to a cruel repressive policy. I have been continuously arrested, and my life has been endangered on multiple occasions.

I have been subjected to torture, arrests and raids on my home by Castro's political police for denouncing the human rights situation in Cuba at international forums.

I am speaking here today on behalf of my brothers and sisters in the internal resistance, as well as of those who are still suffering political imprisonment in Cuba, because of their ideas. Scores of political prisoners remain in Cuban jails in spite of the supposed release of political prisoners carried out by the Castro Regime as a result of the Obama-Castro Accords.

Among my imprisoned brothers are: Ciro Alexis Casanova Perez, Ernesto Borges Perez, Andy Frometa Cuenca and Armando Sosa Fortuny. They are but a few names in a long list of heroes whose sole crime has been to oppose the dictatorship and to continue with their civic resistance from within prison walls.

A few days ago, we learned that the President of this great nation had come to an agreement with dictator Raul Castro. As a result of this agreement, the parties agreed to the establishment of full diplomatic relations, as well as to take steps towards the elimination of US sanctions against the Regime. Three convicted Cuban spies who were serving time in US prisons, one of which actively participated in the murder of American citizens over international waters and all of whom sought to destabilize this country, threatening its national security, were exchanged for imprisoned contractor Alan Gross.

These agreements are considered by a vital segment of the Cuban Resistance as a betrayal of the aspiration to freedom of the Cuban people. They are unacceptable to us. The principles and the right to freedom of a country are not the property of any government, no matter how powerful or influential it is.

There is currently an international effort underway, expressed by the Obama-Castro Accords, to bring about some kind of evolution within the Castro Regime. This idea is simply a farce promoted by the Castro Regime in order to perpetuate itself in power. The Castro dictatorship cannot be reformed. It is based on the rejection of democratic values and everything these stand for. The Castro Regime is a tyrannical regime that seeks not just to control the Cuban people, but also to expand its repression to other countries, as is the case with Venezuela and other Latin American countries.

What would real change look like in Cuba?

It would mean the full restoration of civil rights.
It would mean a general amnesty for all political prisoners.
It would mean recognition of the right to organize independent political parties and labor unions.
It would mean genuine, internationally-supervised free elections.
It would mean separation from power of the Castro brothers.

All of this is recognized in current US law on Cuba policy, and it should remain this way because it constitutes the best type of support for the Cuban Resistance.

Since 1998, a majority of the Cuban Resistance has signed on to the Agreement for Democracy in Cuba, a 10-point roadmap towards a real transition to democracy. We ask recognition from the US Congress for this document and for what it represents as a consensus statement of the Cuban Resistance on the future of our nation.

I ask the people of the United States, as well as this freely-elected Congress, to maintain its firm support for the right of the Cuban people to be free. We may be close to real change in Cuba.

The drop in oil prices, the instability of the Maduro regime in Venezuela, which has been the main sponsor of the Castro dictatorship, as well as the civic resistance which is growing throughout Cuba and important initiatives aimed at coordinating this resistance, as is for example, the Rights and Freedoms Forum, are an example of all this.

This is the moment to demand real changes from the Castro Regime. This means: legalization of independent political parties and labor unions, internationally-supervised free elections, that the Castro brothers are separated from political power, as they have spent decades asphyxiating the Cuban people.

Only this can bring about normal relations between the United States and Cuba. Only this can mean an end to Cubans trying to flee from the island on improvised rafts, only this can mean an end to the exportation of authoritarianism to the rest of Latin America by the Castro Regime. Only this would mean an end to the existence of Cuba as a failed state under a military dictatorship.

Cubans can have the same success in the island that they have had abroad.
What we need is freedom.
The Cuban Resistance is struggling for that freedom.
We need your understanding and support.

Mr. SMITH. Antunez, thank you so very much for that very powerful testimony.

We do have a series of votes on the House floor. We will have to take a short recess.

So, Ms. Soler, if you wouldn't mind, we will just break and then come back for questions.

And I do hope that members of the press and our audience will stay because we have very powerful testimony that awaits.

So we stand in short recess.

[Recess.]

Mr. SMITH. The subcommittee will resume its hearing.

I want to apologize again to our distinguished witnesses for that delay. We did have a series of votes on the House floor. But we are looking forward to your testimony.

We will begin with our second witness, Ms. Berta Soler.

If you could proceed.

STATEMENT OF MS. BERTA SOLER FERNÁNDEZ, LEADER, LADIES IN WHITE (DAMAS DE BLANCO)

[The following statement and answers were delivered through an interpreter.]

Ms. SOLER. Honorable Congressman Smith, distinguished members of the subcommittee, above all, I want to thank you for listening to me and, also, to thank all of the people and organizations who have made it possible for me to testify on the human rights situation in my country, Cuba.

We are presently living through a particularly defining moment for the future of our country in the wake of the recently announced reestablishment of diplomatic relations between Cuba and the United States.

I am appearing here as the leader of the Ladies in White, a group of women activists who support change toward democracy in our country through nonviolent means, inspired by the example of women such as Rosa Parks and Coretta King, among others, who, with courage and determination, blazed paths for full enjoyment of civil rights in this great Nation.

Now, 50 years after the events in Selma, Alabama, and testifying before a subcommittee whose mandate includes global human rights, it is a great honor and historic opportunity for me to appear before you.

I also speak on behalf of numerous leaders and activists from Cuban civil society who have entrusted me with speaking for them before you. It is a civil society that is particularly repressed by the intolerance of a government whose exercise of power consists of the systematic violation of the human rights of the Cuban people.

Just before I left Cuba to be here, last January 28, the day we celebrate the birth of our founding father, Jose Marti, dozens of activists were arrested in Havana and other provinces for attempting to place offerings of flowers at statues of Jose Marti.

In its totalitarian vision, the dictatorship seeks a monopoly on our national identity through use of force against all independent activists. The most respected international human rights organizations have documented violations of human rights in Cuba.

On October 28, 2013, the Inter-American Commission on Human Rights issued an injunction on behalf of the members of Ladies in White to afford protection in the face of systemic repression by Cuban authorities.

I submit the official precautionary measures issued by the Commission for these purposes, as well as a report by Cubalex, which initiated the case before the Commission. I request that these reports be made part of the record of this hearing as documentary evidence for our testimony, as proof of what we are exposing in our testimony today. These documents demonstrate that the subject of political prisoners continues to be one of the most sensitive issues in Cuba today, reaching far beyond occasional or periodic release of some of them.

Resolving this matter requires the unconditional freeing of everyone who has been jailed for political reasons on the island and the elimination of all legal restrictions used to repress those who think differently from the regime.

Cuba continues to be a country with a one-party government where fundamental freedoms that are an absolute right in North American society are crimes against what they regard as state security.

Separation of powers does not exist in Cuba. Freedom of expression and association continue to be repressed, and the Constitution establishes the Communist Party as the driving force for society. The right to strike is regarded as a crime with workers on and off the island, subject to conditions of labor slavery which has been denounced by international organizations at the international level.

While these conditions prevail, it is not possible to speak of a willingness to change on the part of the Castro regime. That same January 28, during his appearance before the third summit of the CELAC held in San Jose, Costa Rica, the dictator Raul Castro stated that Cuba will not give up 1 millimeter.

For us, this signals the continuation of beatings, jailing, forced exiles, discrimination against our children at school, and all manner of patterns of intimidation and abuse that we suffer daily for wanting to see a pluralistic, democratic, and inclusive Cuba.

Our aspirations are legitimate because they are underguided by the Universal Declaration of Human Rights, to which Cuba is a party, and the signed international pacts on civil and political rights which have not been ratified by the dictatorship.

Our demands are quite concrete: Freedom for political prisoners, recognition of civil society, the elimination of all criminal dispositions that penalize freedom of expression and association, and the right of the Cuban people to choose their future through free, plural elections.

We believe these demands are just and valid. Even more importantly, for us, they represent the most concrete exercise of politics, a step in the direction of democratic coexistence.

Cuba will change when the laws that enable and protect the criminal behavior of the forces of repression and corrupt elements that sustain the regime change.

In the name of those that have been executed, in the name of Cuban political prisoners, in the name of the pilots from the humanitarian organization Brothers to the Rescue murdered on the orders of Fidel Castro, in the name of the victims from the March 13 tugboat, in the name of the victims of Cuba's Communist regime, Cuba, yes, Castro, no.

Thank you very much.

[The prepared statement of Ms. Soler follows:]

Berta Soler Testimony, English Translation

Honorable Christopher H. Smith, Chairman of the Subcommittee on Africa, Global Health, Global Human Rights and International Organizations.

This testimony is being delivered in English by Orlando Gutierrez-Boronat

Distinguished Members of the Subcommittee:

Above all, I want to thank you for listening to me and also to thank all of the people and organizations who have made it possible for me to testify on the human rights situation in my country, Cuba. We are presently living through a particularly defining moment for the future of our country in the wake of the recent announced reestablishment of diplomatic relations between Cuba and the United States.

I am appearing here as the leader of the Ladies in White, a group of women activists who support change towards democracy in our country through non-violent means, inspired by the example of women such as Rosa Parks and Coretta King, among others, who with courage and determination blazed paths for the full enjoyment of civil rights in this country. Now 50 years after the events in Selma, Alabama, and testifying before a Subcommittee whose mandate includes Global Human Rights, it is a great honor and an historic opportunity for me to appear before you.

I also speak on behalf of numerous leaders and activists from Cuban civil society who have entrusted me with speaking for them before you. It is a civil society that is particularly repressed by the intolerance of a government whose exercise of power consists of the systematic violation of the human rights of the Cuban people. Just before I left Cuba to be here, last January 28th, the day we celebrate the birth of our Founding Father José Martí, dozens of activists were arrested in Havana and other provinces for attempting to place offerings of flowers at statutes of José Martí. In its totalitarian vision, the dictatorship seeks a monopoly on our national identity through the use of force against all independent activists.

The most respected international human rights organizations have documented violations of human rights in Cuba. On October 23, 2013, the Inter-American Commission on Human Rights issued an injunction on behalf of members of the Ladies in White, to afford protection in the face of systematic repression by Cuban authorities. I submit the official Precautionary Measure issued by the Commission for these purposes, as well as the report submitted to the Commission by the Association of Independent Cuban lawyers (Cubalex) which initiated the case before the Commission. I wish also to submit a report prepared by Cubalex on Cuba's prison system. I request that these reports be made a part of the record of this hearing as documentary evidence for our testimony.

These documents demonstrate that the subject of political prisoners, one of the most sensitive issues in Cuba today, reaches far beyond the occasional or periodic release of some of them. Resolving this matter requires the unconditional freeing of everyone who has been jailed for political reasons on the island and the elimination of all legal restrictions used to repress those who think differently from the regime.

Cuba continues to be a country with a one-party government where fundamental freedoms that are an absolute right in North American society are crimes against what they regard as "State Security."

Berta Soler Testimony, English Translation

Separation of powers does not exist in Cuba, freedom of expression and association continue to be repressed and the Constitution establishes the Community Party as the "driving force" for society. The right to strike is regarded as a crime with workers on and off the island subject to conditions of labor slavery which have been denounced by international organizations. While these conditions prevail, it is not possible to speak of a willingness to change on the part of the Castroite regime.

That same January 28th, during his appearance before the third Summit of the [Community of Latin American and Caribbean States] (CELAC), held in San Jose, Costa Rica, the dictator Raul Castro stated that [Cuba] "...will not give up one millimeter..." of its system of government as negotiations between Cuba and the United States begin, and that it would make no sense to demand that he make changes to a military, dynastic dictatorship that has been in power for more than half a century. For us, this signals the continuation of beatings, jailing, forced exile, discrimination against our children at school, and all manner of patterns of intimidation and abuse we suffer daily for wanting to see a pluralistic, democratic, and inclusive Cuba.

Honorable Mr. Chairman,

Honorable Members of the Subcommittee,

Our aspirations are legitimate because they are undergirded by the Universal Declaration of Human Rights to which Cuba is a party, and the signed international pacts on civil and political rights which have not been ratified by the dictatorship. Our demands are quite concrete: freedom for political prisoners, recognition of civil society, the elimination of all criminal dispositions that penalize freedom of expression and association **and the right of the Cuban people to choose their future through free, multiparty elections.**

We believe these demands are just and valid. Even more importantly, for us they represent the most concrete exercise of politics, a step in the direction of democratic coexistence. Cuba will change when the laws that enable and protect the criminal behavior of the forces of repression and corrupt elements that sustain the regime change.

In the name of those who have been executed.

In the name of Cuban political prisoners.

In the name of the pilots from the humanitarian organization, Brothers to the Rescue, murdered on Fidel Castro's orders.

In the name of the victims from the "March 13th" tugboat.

In the name of the victims of Cuba's Communist regime.

Cuba yes, Castro no.

Thank you very much.

Mr. SMITH. Ms. Soler, thank you very much for that very powerful testimony and for providing very specific benchmarks that the Cuban dictatorship needs to follow if Cuba is truly to be free. Thank you so very, very much.

And I would like to now yield the floor to Ms. Fonseca for such time as you may consume.

STATEMENT OF MS. SARA MARTHA FONSECA QUEVEDO, MEMBER, LADIES IN WHITE (DAMAS DE BLANCO)

[The following statement and answers were delivered through an interpreter.]

Ms. FONSECA. Good morning.

My name is Sara Marta Fonseca Quevedo. I was born in 1970 into a Cuban family that, since 1959, had been branded as a dissident from the state. We were classified as counterrevolutionaries because we were opposed to the incipient Castro regime.

For over half a century in Cuba, the Castro regime has violated and violates human rights. From the beginning, there have been crimes, murders, political prisoners, and people discriminated. All those who speak out against the regime are brutally repressed, imprisoned, or murdered. In spite of having been raised within communism, they were never able to convince us that that is the right way to live.

As a human rights activist, I participated in organizing demonstrations in Havana, among them, a historic demonstration in 2011 in the old Capitol building in the center of Havana. On that day, four women, in spite of repression, opened a banner displaying a slogan calling for the release of all political prisoners.

Hundreds of Cubans witnessed this protest. We inspired many Cubans who began to shout along with us for freedom. Others carried out their own protest. At all times we felt the support of the people. This protest was well worth the repression that we later suffered.

I have been repeatedly arrested. They have beaten me senselessly in police stations to the point that they thought they had killed me. On one occasion, three female police officers dragged me by my hair from one cell to another. While they dragged me by my hair from one cell to the other, they kicked me in my back and in my head.

Once I was in the cell they were taking me to and while I was still handcuffed behind my back, a male police officer kicked me with all his strength in my head. As a result of this, I suffered permanent damage to my right kidney and serious damage to my spinal column. To this day, as a result of this beating, I still suffer from dizzy spells.

It is with this brutality and much worse that the Castro regime controls the Cuban people. They do this to constantly show the people what the cost of rebellion is.

I want to emphasize that this type of repression continues today right now in Cuba. Cubans cannot elect their leaders. Children are indoctrinated in the schools, and those who do not follow the brainwashing cannot finish their studies. The people have been condemned to scarcity, hunger, and misery by the regime.

25

A people without freedom of expression, with all the media controlled by the government, and hungry, are easy to manipulate. People think only about how to feed their family and although they do not like the way they are living, they can only think about survival.

The Cuban people are tired of imposition and dictatorship. In order to escape, they venture out to the sea on makeshift rafts. It is for these reasons that we do not agree with the negotiations between the President of the United States Barack Obama and dictator Raul Castro.

Why negotiate with a dictatorship without taking into account the people and their resistance? What about all the years of suffering, of beatings dealt out by the political police to the opposition and the people when they demanded freedom and democracy? What about the political prisoners, the murdered, the disappeared? What has Raul Castro given in exchange?

Only when all political prisoners are released, only when all independent political parties and labor unions are legalized, only when free multiparty democratic elections are carried out, only when human rights are respected—only then should the embargo be lifted.

I thank God for having been raised by a family which taught me truth, for saying what was on my mind. For stating what was on my mind, I was not able to finish my studies and neither were my sons. My family and I have been repressed, beaten. We have been thrown into cells. My house was destroyed by those using sticks, stones, who hurled all types of paints, tar, waste, excrement, chemical liquids. This attack against my house was carried out by paramilitary thugs hired by the political police.

To lift the embargo means to legitimize dictatorship, to provide them with oxygen so that they stay in power while repressing, jailing, and murdering. The Cuban people will not benefit from lifting of the embargo. Only the regime will benefit. The Castro dictatorship owns every company that exists in Cuba. No Cuban can own their own business. The Castro family owns Cuba.

We have faith in the future of Cuba because we have faith in the struggle of the Cuban resistance. There is only one resistance inside and outside Cuba. The Agreement for Democracy, a historic document signed by a majority of the Cuban resistance, lays out a clear road map toward democracy.

We want freedom, justice, and democracy for Cuba now. God bless Cuba and the United States.

Thank you.

[The prepared statement of Ms. Fonseca follows:]

TESTIMONY OF SARA MARTA FONSECA BEFORE THE SUBCOMMITTEE ON AFRICA, GLOBAL HEALTH, GLOBAL HUMAN RIGHTS, AND INTERNATIONAL ORGANIZATIONS

5 FEBRUARY 2015

This testimony is being delivered in English by Orlando Gutierrez-Boronat

My name is Sara Marta Fonseca. I was born in 1970 . As a leader of the Cuban Resistance, and in spite of the existing repression, I led public protests calling for democracy in my country. In one of these protests, three fellow female activists and myself, members of the Cuban National Civic Resistance Front, led a protesto n the steps of the old Cuban capitol building. This protest was greatly supported by the Cuban people, and sparked wider public protests.

My family had been considered opposed to the Castro Regime since 1959. They were deemed as counter revolutionaries by the Regime for expressing their opposition to Fidel Castro. For more than half a century the Castro Regime has violated and violates human rights, and controlled Cuban national life.

The Castro Regime has confiscated the private businesses of both Cubans and foreigners, transforming the Castro Regime into the sole employer. Crimes such as murder have been carried out against political opponents. Thousands of Cubans have been incarcerated or discriminated against in Cuban society. Any sign of dissent has been brutally persecuted.

Cubans do not have the right to elect their rulers. Children are indoctrinated in their schools. Those who do not comply with this indoctrination cannot finish their studies. The regime has condemned the Cuban people to permanent scarcity, to hunger and poverty. A people deprived of freedom of expression, with all media under control of the state, can be easily manipulated. People think only about how they can feed their families, and although they may not like what they are living through, they only think ahout survival.

Cubans have exiled themselves to different parts around the world, thousands have died trying to cross the Florida Straits. People venture out to sea in makeshift rafts in order to escape from dictatorship and oppression. In Cuba, there are few people left who remember what free presidential elections look like.

It is for all of these reasons that we do not agree with the negotiations between the Obama Administration and the illegitimate Castro Regime. Why negotiate with a dictatorship without taking into account the Cuban people and its Resistance? What about all of these years of suffering? Why should a regime with such a consistent history of repressing its own people be considered a legitimate partner in a negotiation process?

What concession has Raul Castro made? Only when all political prisoners are released, when independent political parties and labor unions can be organized, only when free multiparty elections can be carried out, only when civil rights are fully respected, only then should economic sanctions on the Castro Regime be lifted.

Thousands of my peope have rebelled against the Castro Regime, and paid a very heavy price for doing this. I thank God for having been raised in a family that raised me in freedom. I was not able to finish my university studies because I spoke out against the Regime. My children and family were also discriminated and imprisoned. My house was destroyed by mobs directed by the Regime. My family has suffered both psychological and physical torture, seriously affecting our health.

Ending the US embargo without the Regime freeing all political prisoners, without independent political parties and labor unions being able to organize, without free elections being held, means legitimizing the Castro Regime so that it continues in power, murdering and oppressing the Cuban people.

Ending the US embargo will benefit only the Castro Regime. The Castro family ultimately owns and controls the country's economic life. The Castro family monopolizes Cuban political and economic life. Their permanence in power will benefit only them, and not the Cuban people.

We ask for support for the Cuban Resistance, and for the Agrement for Democracy in Cuba, a consensus document of the Resistance which lays out a ten point program for true democratic change in Cuba. It is in this way that the United States can aid the Cuban people in building a new democratic nation.

––––––––––

Mr. SMITH. Thank you so very much, Ms. Fonseca.

And thank you for reminding us that these atrocities continue to this day, again underscoring the appalling lack of respect for fundamental human rights by the dictatorship.

So thank you for that great testimony.

Mr. Thale, please proceed.

STATEMENT OF MR. GEOFF THALE, PROGRAM DIRECTOR, WASHINGTON OFFICE ON LATIN AMERICA

Mr. THALE. Thank you. I am Geoff Thale, Program Director of WOLA, the Washington Office on Latin America.

I want to thank Chairman Smith and Ranking Member Bass for convening this hearing on these human rights issues in Cuba.

WOLA is a nongovernmental organization. For 40 years, we have done research and advocacy on human rights issues in the Americas. I have followed Latin American human rights issues since the mid-1980s, and I have directed WOLA's Cuba program since 1995.

I travel there regularly. I try to meet with a wide range of Cubans, academics, Catholic and Protestant church leaders, government officials and government critics, government employees, and people in the small business sector.

I have met with the late Oswaldo Paya. I regularly meet with and have met with activists like Elizardo Sanchez. I have had the pleasure of meeting here with visiting Cuban dissidents, including Miriam Leiva and Manuel Cuesta Morua, who spoke in a panel the other day with Ms. Soler in the Senate.

So the question before us today really is: Has the United States squandered an opportunity to promote human rights in Cuba following the December 17 announcement?

And I think our basic position is that, far from squandering an opportunity, our new posture toward Cuba will open new paths to improve the human rights situation and the living conditions of Cubans.

It will provide opportunities to advance U.S. values and interests, opening new avenues of engagement through travel and trade for U.S. citizens, for churches, for academic and cultural institutions and businesses. Overall, it will enhance the prospects for freedom of expression and for reform on the island.

I want to very briefly comment on three issues. One is the human rights situation, the general situation in the country; the second, what I see as the failures of a policy of isolation; and the third, kind of quickly, the opportunities for the ways in which engagement can advance the human rights situation and our interests.

So on the first question, there is very little doubt—and my colleagues on this panel have talked about it—that there are serious human rights problems in Cuba. No one is unrealistic about that, and no one has a rosy view of the situation.

In addition to the human rights situation, I think it is clear that the Cuban economy is overall fairly stagnant. Many people, especially young people, are yearning for real opportunity and don't feel they have it.

And, in fact, the modest economic growth in Cuba in the last few years has led to increases in inequality. And one group in particular that has not benefited from some modest economic growth is Afro-Cuban families and youth.

At the same time, I want to be clear on the other side. The picture in Cuba isn't uniformly grim. Life expectancy in Cuba is about what it is in the United States because of public health measures and medical care.

Literacy levels in Cuba are very high, as high as in the United States overall, reflecting universal public education. Cuba just passed legislation this past summer to prevent discrimination based on sexual orientation.

So very serious problems. But for all its very serious and very real problems, Cubans probably don't face the kind of issues citizens face in a country like Saudi Arabia or other repressive regimes.

So, overall, the question isn't whether there is a real human rights issue in Cuba. Everyone agrees that there is. The question is: What can the United States do to improve that situation?

For the last 55 years, we have pursued a policy of isolation. And I think it is fairly clear, if you hear the testimonies of the other panelists, that policy has failed to do anything to improve the human rights situation on the island.

It has created hardships for Cuban citizens, for normal Cubans. But it has not forced the Cuban Government to change its policies or its direction. And, in fact, in many ways, it has offered the government a rationale to crack down on dissent.

So the policy hasn't succeeded in bringing change in the Cuban Government. At the same time, it has relegated the United States, both U.S. Government and U.S. society, to the sidelines in Cuba itself.

And so, if the policy of isolation has failed—and I think it pretty clearly has—the question is: What about a policy of engagement?

Now, no one thinks a policy of engagement is a magic solution to the human rights problem in Cuba. But I think it is clear that, historically, periods of engagement with Cuba are periods in which we have seen political relaxation, particularly the release of prisoners.

Under President Carter, during the time Pope John Paul II visited, during the 2012 talks with the church and the Spanish Government, all three of them saw significant prisoner releases. And just this past month, following the extensive talks between Cuba and the U.S. Government, 53 political prisoners were released, completing the release of everybody on Amnesty International's list of prisoners of conscience.

So other international actors as well—the Government of Spain, the Government of Canada, the Government of Norway, a number of international groups, including European churches—have seen specific benefits to efforts they have made for engagement with the Cuban Government rather than policies of isolation.

Beyond the dialogue with Cuban officials, I think there are some really important things that greater engagement will do. It will help reformers inside the Cuban system. It will provide them more space and opportunity. It will benefit Cuban families and the Cubans who interact with people-to-people travelers. It is going to benefit religious interaction and expand contact between U.S. and

Cuban churches. Telecommunications is going to offer new opportunities for Internet access and information on the island.

So, overall, I think it is pretty clear that the policy of engagement is likely to expand family visits and remittances, assist a small, but growing, private sector, increase cultural and religious contacts, and help Cubans connect to the outside world. And if the United States is interested in helping ordinary Cubans in promoting democratic values, that is the path we ought to pursue.

We shouldn't be naive in our expectations about Cuba's political leadership. This is the beginning, though, of a long-term process to reduce tension between the governments and build bridges between the American and Cuban people. Over time, that is going to help empower Cuban citizens and open political space on the island.

[The prepared statement of Mr. Thale follows:]

Advocacy for Human Rights in the Americas

Testimony of Geoff Thale
Program Director
Washington Office on Latin America (WOLA)

House Foreign Affairs Committee
Subcommittee on Africa, Global Health, Global Human Rights,
and International Organizations

February 5, 2015

My name is Geoff Thale, and I am the Program Director at the Washington Office on Latin America, WOLA.

WOLA is a U.S. non-profit, non-governmental organization that does research and advocacy to promote human rights in the Americas. Since 1974, WOLA has monitored issues of human rights and democracy in Latin America and has provided information and analysis to congressional offices, presidential administrations, and the general public about conditions in the region and the impact of U.S. policy on human rights. Through strategic collaborations, we partner with courageous people working on social change—advocacy organizations, academics, religious and business leaders, artists, and government officials—and together, we advocate for more just societies in the Americas.

In 1995, I founded WOLA's Cuba program and have directed it ever since. I travel to Cuba every year and have done so since the mid-1990s. I have accompanied multiple congressional delegations to Cuba and have written and spoken extensively about U.S.-Cuba policy and about developments in Cuba itself. I meet with a wide range of Cubans when I visit, including academics, Catholic and Protestant church leaders, government officials, and government critics. I have met with figures such as the late Oswaldo Payá and with well-known human rights activist Elizardo Sánchez. On a recent trip, I met with a young restauraunt owner in Matanzas who is representative of an emerging sector of small businesspeople with their own interests and priorities. I have worked professionally on issues of U.S. foreign policy, human rights, and democracy in Latin America for more than 30 years.

The question before us today is whether the United States has squandered an opportunity to promote human rights in Cuba by normalizing diplomatic relations and undertaking a series of reforms that will increase travel and trade. WOLA believes that when it comes to promoting human rights in Cuba, principled engagement, not unilateral isolation, is the best path forward. Far from squandering an opportunity, the new posture toward Cuba opens new paths to improve the rights situation and living conditions of Cubans in a way that the previous policies simply could not. The new policy provides new opportunities to forward U.S. values and interests. Opening new avenues of engagement through travel and trade for U.S. individual citizens, churches, academic and cultural institutions, and businesses will enhance the prospects for freedom of expression and reform on the island.

Human Rights in Cuba: Different Approaches

My colleagues on this panel have talked about their own situations and about the human rights challenges on the island. They have lived there and can describe their experiences far better than I or other foreign observers can. My expertise is focused on human rights and U.S. policy, and how U.S. policy can most effectively foster human rights improvements.

There's no doubt that Cuba has serious human rights problems. It has only one legal political party. Cuba falls short on international human rights standards on freedom of speech, freedom of the press, and freedom of association. As others on this panel have said, regime opponents are harassed and subjected to arbitrary short-term detentions. These are serious problems to which we should not be indifferent. Cuba should end its restrictions on political parties, freedom of speech, and freedom of assembly.

Perhaps as important to its citizens as the conditions listed above is Cuba's dismal economy. Cuba is a country whose economy is stagnant, and one where many people, especially the young, are yearning for more opportunity. Modest economic growth has led to increases in inequality, and Afro-Cuban families and youth have benefited the least from the changes underway.

To be clear, the picture in Cuba is not uniformly a grim one. Life expectancy is high, reflecting relatively good public health and medical care; literacy levels are high, reflecting universal public education. The country has made some progress on legislation to prevent discrimination based on sexual orientation. For all its very real problems, Cubans do not face the problems that many citizens face in countries such as Saudi Arabia, or other repressive regimes.

The United States and the international community certainly should play a coordinated and constructive role in pressing Cuba to respect and foster human rights. The question that I will examine today, in my capacity as an analyst of U.S. foreign policy and its effect on human rights, is how best to do so, and more specifically, how our new approach of engaging with Cuba will be more effective than our past approach of isolation.

Isolation

The truth is that the last 55 years of embargo have clearly shown that our attempts to isolate Cuba completely failed to improve human rights on the island. The embargo created—and continues to create—hardships for normal Cubans, but it has not forced the Castro regime to reform, nor has it led to a sudden democratic transition in Cuba. In fact, the tensions between the United States and Cuba have long provided the Cuban government with a pretext to crack down on dissent. The U.S. embargo and hostile stance toward Cuba create a "siege mentality" on the island that is trumpeted by official propaganda and used to rationalize limits on freedom of expression.

In the meantime, the Cuban government has begun a transition to a new generation. While it's true that Raúl Castro remains in power, he has announced that he will step down in 2018. His successor, the 54-year-old Miguel Díaz Canel, represents the post-revolutionary generation that will soon be in charge. In addition, a series of economic reforms are underway in Cuba that aim to jumpstart the stagnant Cuban economy. The government has begun to shift large numbers of workers to a newly emerging private sector and incorporate some market mechanisms into its highly centralized and inefficient economic planning system. These economic changes are shifting the foundations of Cuban society, as well as the fundamentals of the relationship between Cubans and their government, for the first time since the 1959 revolution.

None of this is to say that Cuba is about to become a democracy. But it is important to note that these developments are enormously significant in a country in which little has changed in the past five decades.

So as Cuba begins a slow and halting evolution, where is the United States? Under our old policy, the United States—both its government and its citizens—was largely relegated to the sidelines. With little travel and trade and limited diplomatic contact, the U.S. government's concerns could be ignored by Cuba. After more than 50 years without relations, we had none of the relationships or tools of soft power with which to influence Cuba. And U.S. citizens interested in engaging with the Cuban people—be they academics, religious groups, or cultural organizations—were stymied by a labyrinth of regulations and restrictions.

The case for engagement

The normalization of relations with Cuba has been portrayed by some as a series of concessions to the Cuban government. Critics have called it a bad deal, saying that the U.S. betrayed its principles while getting nothing in return from the Cuban government.

But normalizing relations doesn't mean we have taken human rights issues off the agenda with Cuba. In fact, the new policy of conducting direct, high-level talks about a broad range of issues will present greater opportunity to effectively raise human rights concerns.

In fact, every substantial release of political prisoners in Cuba has been linked to periods of engagement, not to increased sanctions. For example, President Jimmy Carter publicly expressed an interest in easing tensions with Cuba, and the Cuban government responded by engaging in a dialogue with Carter on political prisoners—a subject the Cubans had resisted in the past. The negotiations resulted in the release of hundreds of political prisoners to the United States. In 1998, Pope John Paul II visited Cuba and publicly called for political prisoners to be released. In the following weeks, 300 prisoners, including political prisoners, were freed. And in 2010, after decades of acrimony, the Archbishop of Havana, Cardinal Jaime Ortega, and Raúl Castro engaged in series of constructive, mutually respectful discussions about the treatment of dissidents, Church-state relations, and economic and social challenges in Cuba. The Spanish Foreign Ministry, at the time the chief advocate pushing for improving the European Union's relations with Cuba, supported the talks. Ultimately, the dialogue resulted in the release of 110 prisoners, including the last of the 75 dissidents arrested during the "Black Spring" in 2003.

Earlier this month, we learned that 53 prisoners whose cases the United States raised with the Cuban government had been released as a component of the most recent U.S. discussions with Cuba. Short term detentions, though down from their height last year, continue, and we have heard that two of the recently released prisoner have suffered a short term detention. However, our new policy allows the State Department to directly address these and other human rights challenges with the Cuban government.

Other governments have found that engagement strategies have produced benefits. Many of the economists inside Cuba who advocate for internal reform are people who studied abroad, particularly in Canada. Spain's persistent dialogue has yielded movement on political prisoners. Norway's engagement with Cuban civil society has helped support public debates about human rights issues. European church groups have sponsored Cuban partners who run workshops and debates about controversial issues in Cuban society. While engagement is not a silver bullet, the historical evidence is that the Cuban government responds better to dialogue than to ultimatums. The human rights discussions that the United States and other countries have with Cuba will not transform Cuba overnight; however, they may produce some movement on political prisoners, and they open opportunities for dialogue and for more robust relations with Cuban society. They also lay the groundwork for relationships in the future as Cuba evolves.

Beyond dialogue with government officials, the shift in U.S. policy is likely to be beneficial to reformers inside the Cuban official system—in the universities and the churches, among students and the younger generation, in the new private sector—that favor greater openness. As mentioned above, hostility between the United States and Cuba—that is, our old Cuba policy—is used as a justification for crackdowns on internal dissent. As those tensions slowly dissipate, we expect to see internal dialogue and public debate grow in Cuba. Reform-minded individuals and groups will be more empowered to speak and act in this new context.

People-to-people exchanges and Cuban-American family travel have helped Cuban families stay connected with their relatives in the United States and receive much-needed economic support. Increased travel to Cuba also supports the growing private sector; many U.S. travelers stay in privately run bed-and-breakfasts, eat in private restaurants, and take private taxis. These travelers put money directly into the hands of ordinary Cubans. People-to-people travelers also engage a broad range of Cubans in dialogue with people from the United States about politics, the economy, press freedom, health care, and a range of other issues. These dialogues help encourage new thinking in Cuba and expose Cubans to the outside world. Again, our old policy put unnecessary restrictions on Americans' ability to travel to Cuba to make connections with ordinary Cubans.

The new Cuba policy will also allow for U.S. travelers to provide technical assistance, training, and goods to Cuban entrepreneurs and cooperatives, who often lack basic inputs and business know-how. Increased remittances will permit individuals, families, and organizations to set up small businesses, NGOs, and other organizations that will function in a newly open space for small business and other groups in Cuba. The growth of these organizations and this political space is an important and positive step, and it will inevitably produce movement in Cuba for greater change and more openness.

A key part of the new policy is to allow U.S. telecommunications companies to operate in Cuba, thus expanding internet access on the island. Increasing internet access within Cuba will help break down barriers to communication and expand citizens' ability to get information and engage in debate.

The reforms the U.S. has made will allow greater flows of non-fmaily remittances and create a general license for sending building supplies to Cuba. This will allow our own church communities to deepen their ties to Cuban churches.

Family visits and remittances, assisting a growing private sector, expanding cultural and religious contacts, helping Cubans connect to the outside world—if the United States is interested in helping ordinary Cubans and promoting democratic values, why would it be U.S. policy to restrict any of these types of activities?

This kind of engagement will not, of course, magically transform Cuba overnight. What it will do is open contact and dialogue with the whole spectrum of Cuban society. That includes the Catholic church, which has supported this new approach, with the Protestant churches and the Jewish community. It includes the small business owners who are opening bed and breakfasts and restaurants, and performing other service jobs. It includes the university professors, and the students, who want to talk informally about their society and about ours. It includes the medical workers and health care professionals and the scientific researchers.

In that kind of dialogue and engagement, which will develop over time as the new U.S. policy is implemented, lies the future of Cuba.

As I've said before, change will not come overnight. My colleagues on this panel and others like them will continue to face difficulties and challenges. But this is the beginning of a long-term process to build bridges between the American and Cuban people. We shouldn't be naïve in our expectations about the political leadership in Cuba. But over time, engagement will help empower Cuban citizens and open political space in Cuba.

———————

Mr. SMITH. Thank you very much for your testimony.

We are joined by a member of the subcommittee who had a previous engagement at the opening part of this hearing, Mr. Clawson, the gentleman from Florida. So I yield time for his opening statement.

Mr. CLAWSON. Thank you. Thank you for coming today.

Mr. Thale, I want to start by thanking you for coming.

I just want to say for the record I am in a bit of a disagreement here. I think that, if foreign direct investment was a good way to get these folks to come around, we would be in a better place right now.

The Spaniards have had nice hotels on Varadero for a long time and it just hasn't had enough of an impact. And so I am worried that we are just casting a lifeline to murderous folks that were really about to go under.

Senor Garcia, Senora Solera and Senora Fonseca, bienvenidos.

[Speaking foreign language.]

You have my full admiration, my full respect, [speaking foreign language] for what you are doing and the fight that you are waging, an example not only for your country, but for my countrymen as well.

And anything that I can do to help you in this sacred fight, I am willing and enthusiastic to do so. I am so sad, sometimes brokenhearted, for your suffering and your injuries,and I can't imagine what it would be like.

[Speaking foreign language.]

And so I want to tell you wholeheartedly how much I support what you are doing.

[Speaking foreign language.]

Mr. SMITH. Mr. Clawson, thank you so very, very much.

If you would like to respond—Ms. Bass does have a plane to catch and asked if she could say a few words.

Ms. BASS. Yes. Thank you, Mr. Chairman.

And thank the witnesses for their testimony.

I have a couple of questions. I sit on the board of the National Endowment for Democracy, and there is about 27 organizations that are funded to help with activists in Cuba. Some of the organization are funded in Cuba and some of them are funded in Miami. I just wondered, one, if you thought that the funding was helpful.

And then, also, the three of you are here today, and I just wondered how you were able to come—are you here for a long time?— or how you were able to get out of Cuba. Do you travel back and forth?

Those are the questions I wanted to ask the three of you. And then I would like to direct a question to the other witness.

Ms. FONSECA. Yes. All types of aid received by the opposition in Cuba is very important. I can tell you that, thanks to the aid we have received in Cuba, we have been able to save at least one life. And I will give you an example.

When you have a cell phone in your hand, you have a weapon with which to defend yourself. Without the aid we get from abroad, we couldn't pay for that cell phone. On many occasions, we have been able to transmit from one corner of the island to the other about an activist who has disappeared or been arrested who otherwise there would be no news about. And thanks to that kind of communication, we are able to go out into the streets and to demand freedom for those who have been arrested.

Ms. BASS. You know, I am relatively new on the board. So I was just learning about the funding. But given that we don't even have mail exchange—not much, I don't think—between our two countries, I was surprised that you were even able to get any aid from the United States.

Ms. FONSECA. Yes. It is very clear that you can receive aid from one family member to another. That is why the Cuban exile community is so important.

Ms. BASS. And then, also, about your travel, are you able to go back and forth between the—I mean, I know you are here today for this. I don't know if you have been here for a while. But you are able to go back and forth?

Ms. FONSECA. In my case, I am a refugee in the United States.

Ms. BASS. Okay. I see.

But you guys are going back. Right? Didn't you mention that you were——

Ms. SOLER. At this moment in time, some activists are able to leave Cuba and come back thanks to the aid that we receive from some NGOs. This doesn't mean we are free, because there are many activists who are impeded from leaving Cuba by the regime.

Ms. BASS. Sure. No. I mean, I was just surprised anybody was—you know, I understand, especially financially. But the fact that you were able—because they know what you are doing. Right?

Ms. SOLER. I want to give you an example. There are former political prisoners—there are at least 12 former political prisoners who are part of a larger group of 75 who were released from prison that are still under house arrest and they can't leave Cuba.

And I give you a more recent example. One of the Ladies in White, Sonia Alfonso Alvarez, she was released on December 9 and, when she went to request her passport, it was denied to her.

I label the change that Raul Castro did in 2013 as a petty reform. As long as they can determine who leaves, who enters, there is no freedom to travel.

Ms. BASS. Okay. And then, finally—because I promised the chair I would be quick—I wanted to ask, Mr. Thale, if you could talk about some of the—in the President's proposals, it is going to allow more economic exchange between our two countries.

And I am wondering what impact you think that might have, especially on the freedom or lack thereof, of people to open up their own businesses. I mean, I understand there is some businesses, like people that have restaurants in their homes and stuff like that. I don't know to what extent there is extensive free enterprise.

But do you think that that is ultimately going to assist the development of that?

Mr. THALE. Thank you for the question, Congresswoman.

So Cuba in 10 years ago, about 90 percent of the population of the Cuban workforce worked for state or state businesses. Today that is probably down to about 70 percent.

The number of people who work for themselves in small businesses has gone up from about 150,000 4 years ago to about ½ million now. So there has been a substantial increase.

Some of those businesses are quite successful and have a dozen, 15 employees. The vast majority of them are small vendors, small restaurants, people selling and dealing out of their home.

I think that the opening we have offered to the private sector—it is going to take a while for that to work through. But it is clear that it will strengthen the capacity of those businesses and the creation of a small private business sector. I think we will see change in that area over time.

Ms. BASS. Thank you.

I yield back my time.

Mr. SMITH. Thank you, Ms. Bass.

First of all, let me introduce Basilio Guzman, who was a political prisoner for 22 years and was subjected to heinous torture, unbelievable acts for brutality.

Thank you for joining us at today's hearing and for your courage.

I would also like to introduce Iris Tamara Perez Aguilera, who is the wife of Antunez, if you would, and a leader in her own right. She founded the Rosa Parks Civil Rights Movement and has spoken out bravely along with her husband.

Thank you for joining us at today's hearing as well.

I would like to ask a few opening questions and then yield to my distinguished colleagues.

First of all, if you could, Mr. Antunez, if you wouldn't mind, speaking to the issue of the mistreatment of Afro-Cubans.

I have learned over the last several years—and I have been working on Cuban rights issues—I have been in Congress 35 years. I have been working on Cuban human rights issues for 35 years. But there has been, I think, a lack of attention given to the additional mistreatment endured by Afro-Cubans.

All people who aspire to freedom and democracy, the full weight of tyranny comes down upon them. But there also seems to be a further differentiation and focus—negative bias—prejudice against Afro-Cubans.

If you could speak to that.

Mr. GARCIA. I appreciate your concern and your interest that all of you have shown today for the cause of Cuba, and I appreciate that concern even from those who are in agreement with Barack Obama's policy.

Before I answer your question directly, I would like to reflect on something. And with all due respect for one of the panelists, I felt great pain a few moments ago.

I felt ill at ease to listen from you that the Cuban situation is bad, but not that bad, the situation in Cuba is bad, but not that bad. I really don't understand, with all due respect, what you mean by a situation that is bad, but not that bad.

And when you say this, I think about Cuban mothers who go to sleep crying because they have no food for their kids the next day. I think of those thousands of young women who have had to become prostitutes so they can feed their families. I think of the fact that Cubans can barely afford to live. I think about the gross inequality between the regime leaders and the people. I think about the moral, spiritual, and economic poverty of the people of Cuba.

There may be some educational achievement in Cuba, but we are talking about a system of education which consists of indoctrination. When all three of us who are here were discriminated from pursuing higher education as youth because we had different political ideas, I think that invalidates, with all due respect, your argument.

It is true Cuba is a medical power. But Cuba is not a medical power for Sara Marta Fonseca, for Berta Soler, or for Jorge Luis Garcia Perez.

Cuba has many sophisticated hospitals and clinics which are first world-class. But those clinics, like the Fiera del Silla and Simex, are only for people who can pay with dollars. They are only for tourists or for the elite.

I also heard you say that the human rights situation is not that grievous. How hard it must be for someone like Sidro Alexis Garcia to listen to—is it not that bad to be in prison merely for displaying a sign and calling for freedom?

Is it not that bad to be in prison like Ernesto Borges? And I want to emphasize this case. Mr. Barack Obama released three confessed spies from the U.S. who were conspiring against the stability and the security of this country. However, this young man was sentenced to 30 years in prisonand he spent 18 years in prison because he passed on information to the U.S. about 26 Cuban spies who were being sent to the U.S. to conspire against the U.S. It is not that Cuba's situation is not that bad. It is extremely bad.

And if you will allow me, I want to comment on your reflection and I want to address directly what you asked.

I want to ask: Why is it that you can't go into Cuba? Why is it that you can't travel to Cuba? Because if you are allowed to go into a Cuban prison, all you will see are black people, hundreds of black men. You will see men who would rather jump from a rooftop and commit suicide or you will see men being bitten by dogs. You will see the beatings. You will see the persecution. You will see these very far-flung sentences, these very high sentences. You will see dozens and dozens of political prisoners who weren't even mentioned in these negotiations.

If you want to go to Cuba, simply tell them that you are not going to visit prisons and that you don't want to meet with dissidents.

I think this addresses what you asked about discrimination in Cuba.

Mr. SMITH. Mr. Antunez, thank you very much.

You know, the Washington Post has done several editorials very, very critical of President Obama's moving toward opening up diplomatic relations or further relations. And they made a very, very salient point that I would just like to underscore here, and that is that we are repeating mistakes that have been made in the past.

When Bill Clinton went to Vietnam and opened up relations with Vietnam, which followed very quickly with the Bilateral Trade Agreement under President Bush, many of us said it was a mistake not to get human rights reforms, durable reforms, first and then move to the diplomatic recognition, followed by an economic relationship.

The Post points out that it is the way Mr. Obama has gone about this that is a mistake, not reform first, but moving in to provide a lifeline, as one of their editorials pointed out—a lifeline to a dictatorship at a time when Venezuela is less capable to provide funding.

And we know that several years ago that funding from what was then the Soviet Union ceased to exist. A very opportune time to press the case for human rights and we blew it when it came to Vietnam.

I have had passed in this Congress, three Congresses and counting, the Vietnam Human Rights Act. Harry Reid, the majority leader, now minority leader, would not put it up for a vote. But three times bipartisan legislation with clear benchmarks toward Vietnam because they are in a race to the bottom with China and North Korea.

Cuba is already there. And, yet, having not learned a single lesson from those failed openings where they get stronger, the dictatorship becomes further empowered.

I firmly disagree, Mr. Thale, with your comment about isolation. We are talking about financially enabling a lifeline, to quote the Washington Post.

And one of their editorials was President Obama's betrayal of Cuban Democrats. Many of those—some have already been re-arrested that were let out. And, of course, as I pointed out, there were just under 200 that we know of that have been arrested in the last several weeks alone.

So that has been the game that Fidel Castro plays. He lets people in and out, but always has this sword of Damocles hanging over the entirety of this dictatorship.

But I have a question, if I could, on an issue. And then I will yield to my good friend and colleague, Chairwoman Ileana Ros-Lehtinen.

I have been working and I am a leader in the area of combatting human trafficking. I am the prime author of what is known as the Trafficking Victims Protection Act of 2000. It is our landmark law to combat modern-day slavery.

Well, the State Department has a Trafficking in Persons office created by my law. And they put out an annual listing of countries using what we contained in the law called minimum standards. The worst designation is Tier 3.

Cuba, again, is a Tier 3 country, an egregious violator of trafficking with full complicity of the Castro brothers and the rest of that government, making money hand over fist by forcible prostitution and by child prostitution.

In 2004, Frank Calzon had documentation and was working on the Human Rights Commission in Geneva. He had documentation of the complicity of this dictatorship with child prostitution and child exploitation. And he was knocked out cold, hit in the face, by Cuban so-called diplomats, thugs.

Freedom House came to his defense and made a very strong statement against it because he was bearing witness to that ugly truth of child prostitution. And, again, the State Department chronicles this. Cuban citizens have been subject to forced prostitution outside of Cuba as well. And then child prostitution and child sex tourism continues.

In the hotels that were mentioned by Mr. Clawson and other places, renting children, that is the reality of what this barbaric regime is all about. They make money by child sex tourism. Again, it is not an open society. I would love for investigators to be able to go there and, of course, look to bring charges against those, including higher-ups in the government. Tier 3 country.

I would like to ask any of our witnesses if they would like to speak to the despicable record of Cuba when it comes to the modern-day slave trade.

Ms. SOLER. It is very important for you to know that the Cuban Government promotes child prostitution in Cuba. The Cuban Government knows that there are many youths who don't go to school, but who are on the streets looking for ways to make money to feed their families.

It is shameful to say, but I must say just last week there was a group of young women saying that they were organizing themselves and preserving themselves for when American tourism arrives so they can sell themselves to American tourists.

If we call the prostitution of hundreds of Cuban youths empowerment, if we call Cubans who are going to try and steal and take from their places of work in order to feed their families—if we call this empowerment, if we call empowerment that women, like the Ladies in White, who go out in the streets to demand freedom and respect for human rights and are beaten—if we call this empowerment, if we call empowerment the Castro regime filling schools with teachers who are poorly trained, the children of human rights activists are failing their tests, and they are damaged or harmed in their studies because their parents are involved in human rights activity, this is not what we want for Cuba.

The Cuban Government is trying to build a Chinese model in Cuba. The Cuban regime wants oxygen and needs air. The Cuban Government wants a capitalist economic system and a Communist political system. We can't tolerate this after over half a century. Human rights first. Economy second.

The Cuban people are suffering, hungry, not because of the American Government. The Cuban people are hungry because the Communist system doesn't work.

We don't want a succession in Cuba. We don't want a continuation of the regime. We don't want a dynasty in power. We want free elections. The resources that are meant for the Cuban people, Raul Castro will take to strengthen the repressive apparatus. Thank you.

Mr. SMITH. I yield to the chairwoman, Ileana Ros-Lehtinen.

Ms. ROS-LEHTINEN. Thank you so much, Mr. Smith. Thank you for calling this important hearing. Thank you to our witnesses, who are victims of the Castro regime, for being here today.

Antunez, Berta, Sara, Iris, I am humbled to be in your presence. Some of you live in Cuba. Others are here now but have family in Cuba so I know that you are very brave for being here today.

This is sort of an insurance policy that you have offered them, Mr. Smith, because by being here today, perhaps they will have some degree of protection that those other figures, as brave as you are, won't have. So I know you worry about them. Thank you for holding up their photos.

Thank you for describing the current dismal human rights situation in my native homeland of Cuba. And I wanted to just give this statement and then ask you some questions.

How has the regime's treatment of its critics changed since December 17th? Do you think this announcement will force changes? I will ask you to respond in a minute.

How does the regime manipulate the press here in the United States and elsewhere and visitors and tourists on the island that may come back here with a distorted picture of what is going on? This morning, I did a radio interview, and the reporter says, "I know Cuba; I was there for a week."

Antunez and Berta, you will hear—you have heard from some today that Castro's Cuba is a picture of equality, that the regime supports everyone's rights, including the rights of Afro-Cubans. Thank you for pointing out the kind of apartheid government that exists there, especially the medical apartheid and the prison apartheid. Thank you for pointing out the mistreatment of the Afro-Cubans.

And, Mr. Thale, you testified that the picture in Cuba is not a uniformly grim one. The fact that you essentially say, "Hey, look, it could be worse," I suppose so. It can always be worse. And it is particularly disgusting and it is an affront to the panelists who sit beside you and the countless number of people who have been jailed for expressing their God-given and fundamental human rights, to thousands who have died trying desperately to flee Cuba.

This is such a workers' paradise where the situation is not that bad that I have people—I see people in my district that wash ashore trying to flee Castro's Cuba. Even now, as all of these negotiations have taken place, there is a 40-percent increase in the number of Cubans fleeing this situation that is "not that bad." People who live in constant fear because the regime is watching them closely or the millions more who have managed to flee over the years.

You are repeating the Castro propaganda about good public health care. These are the constituents that I represent now. They fled Cuba. You should come to Miami and meet with my constituents and have them tell you about this great medical care. I have seen it in the Michael Moore documentary, "Sicko." Where does that exist? Where is that medical care for these folks?

I know that if you are a tourist, you will certainly be treated well. It is good propaganda. Public education, advancement of LGBT rights. The real truth is that the good medical care is just a show for the Castro regime reserved only for the regime officials and the tourists. I know because I represent that community. My district is overwhelmingly Cuban-Americans. I don't know how I got elected. It is just a fluke, I guess. But these are the folks who vote for me and will vote for Mario and vote for Carlos Curbelo, vote for Marco Rubio, vote for Bob Menendez and Albio Sires.

But we know that the system of medical in Cuba, for all, most vast majority of Cubans, they have no access to this system. Please interview the people as they get off the planes from Cuba. Dr. Oscar Elias Biscet, thrown in jail for disclosing the truth about abortions being committed and the poor hospital conditions. And Mr. Smith has brought that out time and time again.

Life expectancy rates and other healthcare statistics in Cuba, where do we get those from? You are doing a survey in Cuba? They are manipulated by the regime. It is unbelievable that we swallow this.

And you have fallen into the trap, Mr. Thale, that Castro set for you, willing to swallow the regime propaganda, spread it to them to give it legitimacy. They are utter falsehoods and repeated over and over again to the detriment of the truth, of the public, and especially the Cuban people.

It is such a great system, the public education system. As these witnesses have pointed out, it is a public indoctrination program. Have you seen the textbooks? Meant to stymie free thinking and free will.

Progress on sexual discrimination? Please, I have met with prominent Cuban LGBT advocates, Wendy Iriepa Padilla and Ignacio Estrada Cepero, and they have vigorously dismissed the claims of progress on LGBT. They have condemned the continual denial of human rights for everyone. The Castro regime will project LGBT rights if you agree with the Castro regime. They will protect anyone who agrees with the Castro regime. But be an LGBT individual in Cuba and speak out against the regime, see how far that gets you.

So my first question to you, Mr. Thale, is: Can you honestly look at your copanelists in the eye and tell them that the picture in Cuba isn't a particularly grim one—it is not that bad—and that the torture, the beatings, the imprisonment, the harassment that they have had to endure isn't particularly grim?

Your 17 years in prison, not particularly grim, not that bad. The beatings of Ladies in White, including 13 who were detained on Sunday, but the press doesn't cover that anymore because they want to have their bureau in Havana. And you talk about how the engagement has led to the release of political prisoners. You point to this false list of 53 as part of the December 17th announcement. But what happens the next day when we are not looking, when people aren't looking for Cuba, when the press has done their standups and they have got their bureau? They don't want to lose that bureau. Oh, no. How many more of these dissidents are rearrested? How many more are detained?

How many more—how many of the 53 have been released prior to the agreement, or are you under the fallacy that that 53 list is authentic? Haven't some of them been rearrested? And what about those other ones who never made it to the list? Why 53? There were 9,000 imprisoned last year, according to reports. And how about those individuals that Mr. Antunez held up? What has happened to them?

The modus operandi of the regime is to do this bait and switch, to release some prisoners out of expediency, to promulgate its propaganda and then, when the spotlight is off, rearrest those people or find new ones to throw in jail. But now they don't even have to wait until the press attention is out.

Like I said, just on Monday, a young rapper was put in jail for a year for dangerousness which could lead to a crime. How can you justify that? How can you say, oh, we have liberated these 53, and it is not that bad?

I want to ask you—to our panelists here: Mr. Antunez, has it not been that bad for you? When you were in jail, not that bad? Not that grim?

And Berta and Sara.

Mr. GARCIA. I think that the situation with the violation of human rights in Cuba is much worse than we can describe. It has been written about in some documentaries that have been made. But none of them capture the full reality. They can't capture the brutal reality of imprisonment in Cuba.

Maybe those who don't have a real good idea or don't have all the information about what a Cuban prison is like could come to think that a prisoner in Cuba is merely deprived of their freedom. They could ignore that Cuban political prisoners are injected with water and told that they are being injected with some kind of sedative. There have been cells throughout Cuban prisons where murders and beatings have taken place. There have been clinically induced suicides which have taken place in Cuban prisons.

I will never forget Samuel Simpson Gonzalez when he was manipulated by the prison authorities to jump off a third-story rooftop. I will never forget the use of Shakira, a device for torture, in Cuba. I don't want to consume too much of your time telling you about all the horrors of the prisons because I have so many examples of torture that we wouldn't have enough time for me to go over all of them.

If you ask me how I could describe political imprisonment in Cuba, I would ask you to ask Dante and find it in his great work. You can't talk about process of engagement, of dialogue, of understanding if you ignore something as important, as crucial, as essential as political prisoners.

We often talk about the embargo, and we hear it mentioned in different forums. Eloquent voices speak out against the embargo. However, one of the Members of Congress who is not present right now, blames the embargo for not being able to go to Cuba. But it should be mentioned—perhaps they should mention that the only real embargo, the only real blockade that the Cubans face is the cruel criminal Castro dictatorship that does not limit itself and on a weekly basis beats women on the streets, a regime who murdered in the hospital a courageous woman like Ladies in White founder Laura Pollan or who murdered Orlando Zapata Tamayo by not letting him drink water for 18 days.

Yeah, there will be changes. There will be improvements, but not for the people. It will be for that regime that has imprisoned so many Cubans, that has repressed Cubans, and that is frankly taking the lead in these negotiations.

Those of us who are sitting here are not extremists. We are not backward-looking people. We are not against policies of engagement and understanding. And we think that the best way to solve a conflict is by approaching. But what we can't accept is that you confuse Cuba with the regime that oppresses Cuba. What we will not accept and we have no reason to accept is that the Cuban opposition be ignored in these negotiations.

The Castro regime has found in Barack Obama's engagement policy part of the incentives it needs in order to continue repressing. In order to maintain itself in power, as well as to legitimatize itself internationally, these accords have been very strong. The Cuban resistance does not recognize these accords, and we do not count for moral authority or executive authority, no matter how powerful they may be.

We are appreciative of international solidarity, and we accept it. We respect those who think that President Obama's policies will benefit Cuba. But all that we ask, please, is that you recognize us and that you take us into account.

Ms. ROS-LEHTINEN. Berta.

Ms. SOLER. It is very important for you to know that the Cuban Government uses state terrorism against defenseless women. The Cuban Government is not a sovereign government. The Cuban Government has not been elected. Therefore, we Cubans are the sovereignty of Cuba. We have the right to express our opinion.

It is very important that you know we have no problem with the Government of the United States because they have always tried to support the people of Cuba. What we are against is the way in which these negotiations are being conducted because we are the sovereignty of the people of Cuba.

The secrecy surrounding the list of political prisoners who were going to be released was another deceit of the Cuban Government. Fourteen prisoners had already been released. But these 14 were not free men like those three spies that President Obama unconditionally handed over to the Castro regime. These political prisoners that were released by Castro regime have been released on parole.

You must take us into account. We can help in how the U.S. Government deals with the Cuban Government. You can't do business with criminals, and if you do, you must have conditions.

You can see how Raul Castro himself is already setting conditions. But which are the conditions that we are demanding from the Cuban Government? How can it be possible that so much violence is exerted against women simply because they are trying to practice their religious freedom?

How can it be possible that you are peacefully walking on a sidewalk in your country and the regime hurls pro-government thugs, paramilitary thugs against you? How can it be possible that the police take us to faraway parts of the city and that they fracture our wrists with their pistol butts?

It is a suffering people. It is a people that needs freedom. Freedom depends on us Cubans, but we need the material and spiritual support of other governments.

I am going to go further back. In 1980, 100,000 Cubans left Cuba—teachers, engineers, physicians. Castro called them scum and said they were leaving due to economic reasons.

Ms. ROS-LEHTINEN. Now, Berta, I am going to interrupt you a second because I know that you have got a flight to catch. I just want to say something before you leave.

This is the news from today: ''Dissidents Arrested for Protest Near Cuban National Assembly this Morning.'' So much has changed. A group of 12 dissidents were arrested as they tried to stage a protest near the Havana headquarters of the Cuban regime's National Assembly. The dissidents, part of the Orlando Zapata Tamayo Civil Resistance Front took out a sign demanding the elimination of Castro's draconian laws—that ever wonderful social dangerousness—and the ratification of the U.N. human rights covenants. Their whereabouts remain unknown.

In stark contrast, this release says, Cuban democracy activists Jorge Luis Garcia Perez, Antunez, and Sara Martha Fonseca, both leaders of this group, are freely and openly testifying before the U.S. House of Representatives in Washington, DC, this morning. What a contrast.

Berta, you have got to hop on a plane. And I know that you will be marching with the Ladies in White on Sunday. We will pray for you. We will pray for all of the people of Cuba. You make us proud. You make freedom and liberty shine.

[Speaking foreign language.]

Ms. SOLER. [Speaking foreign language.]

Ms. ROS-LEHTINEN. Thank you so much. Thank you. Now move your butt over to the airport. Because that is free commerce in action, they won't hold that plane. Only in Castro's Cuba will they hold it.

[Speaking foreign language.]

Sara, and then I don't know if Mr. Thale could speak as well.

[Speaking foreign language.]

Ms. FONSECA. If you allow me, I would like to speak about the private sector in Cuba. There is no private sector in Cuba—where there is no freedom to negotiate. The so-called cuentapropistas or self-entrepreneurs, who are a very tiny minority, are constantly blackmailed and manipulated by the regime.

They must respond to the interest of the regime in order to keep their businesses running. They can't have their own unions. They can't defend their rights. That is why I insist, no type of commerce with Cuba benefits the people. Whatever money enters Cuba remains in the hands of the regime.

I also want to say I feel a deep sadness every time I think of political prisoners. It is very hard that in the 21st century, there are still people in my country who are imprisoned for their ideas, that there are so many marginalized people who can't even finish their studies because of their ideas. But it is not only this. Many youth who are not directly involved in opposition activity also suffer from persecution and also suffer from discrimination because they are the children of opposition activists. It is a crime that youth cannot pursue their studies and that they desperately seek in prostitution a means of which to maintain their families.

We condemn the Castro regime. We demand that there be no impunity for the regime. We want a free, just, and democratic country.

Ms. ROS-LEHTINEN. Thank you so much.

And, Mr. Chairman, I regret that I have a plane to catch as well. I did not give Mr. Thale a chance to respond. I don't know if you will be able to, and I will hear it on C–SPAN radio.

Mr. SMITH. Thank you. Thank you so very much.

Ms. ROS-LEHTINEN. Thank you so much. Thank you. I am on Berta's flight, I just remembered. It is not going to wait for me either. Thank you, sir.

Mr. SMITH. Thank you.

Mr. Thale.

Mr. THALE. Only briefly. Thank you. Thank you for the series of questions and comments.

Without wanting to enter into a whole debate about exactly how you characterize the human rights situation in Cuba, which I don't think is particularly profitable, I think it is clear—no one denies that there are serious human rights problems on the island. The question is how to address them and what the United States Government can do. And I think that the policy of engagement that was announced on the 17th—the policy has been supported by others in the Cuban dissident community, some of who testified before the Senate the other day, that is supported by the Catholic Church in Cuba, that is supported by the U.S. Catholic Conference, that was endorsed by the Pope, that a number of Republicans as well as Democrats in this Congress have endorsed, that Freedom House has endorsed—I think the message is there is a very strong view that the best way to address the human rights situation in Cuba is engagement.

Mr. SMITH. Thank you, Mr. Thale.

Let me just—and I will give—if any of you want to make any final comments as we conclude the hearing.

I will, again, respectfully disagree, Mr. Thale. And I thank you for your candor.

We have tried that before, and it seems to me it is not about isolation. It is about meaningful engagement where steps that we take are predicated on just observing universally recognized human rights. We are only asking that the Universal Declaration of Human Rights, the treaties that have been enacted, for want of a better word, with concurrence and full all-in by the countries of the world—be followed and certainly the convention against torture, which has been violated with impunity by Castro and is one of the most egregious violations. Torturing people is one of the most heinous acts one human being can commit against another.

I would just very quickly, Mr. Thale, have you ever asked to meet with a political prisoner in prison?

Mr. THALE. [Shakes head no.]

Mr. SMITH. No? I hope you would. I have made it my business, in 35 years as a Member of Congress, to meet with dissidents everywhere and anywhere I go where there is a repressive regime. But I always seek to go to the prisons to try to show some solidarity, some empathy with those who are suffering the daily acts of torture and brutal mistreatment that Mr. Antunez articulated.

You know, the book that got me into fighting for religious freedom, frankly, in 1981 was "Tortured for Christ," by Richard Wurmbrand, who talked about the Securitate and, just like in the prisons of Cuba, where torture is commonplace. And then when I read Armando Valladares' book, as I mentioned earlier, he talked about these tortures that just never ended. He even talked about Ho Chi Minh poles that would be jabbed as people tried—and there was no sleep. Talk about sleep deprivation. Just no sleep. But you never know when you are going to get another shot in the face, the nose, the solar plexus, the groin area, as the guards shifted from one guard shift to another. They would use these Ho Chi Minh poles. And then the—some of the things that Mr. Antunez talked about always designed by sadists to get the worst—extract the worst possible pain on women and men and then, of course, the sexual abuses that are visited upon people as well.

Dr. Biscet talked about how they punched his teeth. You know, major, major problems. Just beatings, beatings, and more beatings. I honestly believe Castro and those who have committed these atrocities ought to be held to account by the world for crimes against humanity rather than invited in as partners.

Yes, you have got to deal with dictators as a country. Ours does, as do many others. But to have human rights as, you know, an issue, maybe an issue, not THE issue, is a serious mistake.

And again, the embargo, I would just say for the record—and perhaps some of our witnesses want to speak to this—there has been robust trade with the European Union, Canada, and other countries of the world with Cuba for decades. And there has been no diminution whatsoever in torture, child sex trafficking. If anything, the trade has facilitated, particularly with convicted pedophiles and others who travel the world to abuse little children, to rent a boy or a girl when they go to Cuba. I just had passed on the floor of the House of Representatives for the third time the International Megan's Law. So that convicted pedophiles—that we will notice countries of destination when they are leaving to go on sex tourism trips. How horrific is it that the Government of Cuba actually benefits financially from that. And if that is not accurate, then, allow a full-scale investigation because we have so many stories and so much information. And, again, I have to say this—and I will put this, major parts of this into the record—the Trafficking Victims Protection Act has established—will be called the TIP Report. It comes out every year. And Cuba, again, has been designated an egregious violator, a Tier 3 country when it comes to modern day slavery.

So, you know, the idea of trade and somehow there will be a matriculation with more trade with a dictatorship toward democracy didn't work in Vietnam. They have gotten worse. Has not worked in China. Xi Jinping is in a love affair with Mao Zedong. He longs for the day of the Mao, and he is taking that country further down the road of torture as more trade occurs with the People's Republic of China.

And even many of our businesses are learning that if you don't respect human rights, intellectual property rights and the like are another casualty of a dictatorship.

And when people talk about the Internet being open, I am the one who held the hearings right in this room several times, but one truly historic one with Google, Yahoo, Microsoft, and Cisco—and, yes, it was in China. Swore them all in, and they were part of the censorship.

And we know the Castro regime has great capabilities, as does Lukashenka in Belarus, as do other dictators to ensure that that Internet and—whether it be emails or anything else will be very closely surveilled so that more of the best and the bravest and the brightest of Cuba are found and apprehended and thrown into prisons. So there is no open Internet there. There isn't in any dictatorship anywhere in the world. China has literally written the book on how a dictatorship can control the Internet with the great firewall of China. And we have a situation that will replicate itself big time there.

Finally, I would just say this testimony from these unbelievably brave women and men who have suffered at the hand of Castro helps tear off the veil of secrecy, an open secret, if you will; it has been out there. But, thankfully, through C–SPAN and the media that is here and the Congressmen and women who will see this record, you are bearing truth and bearing witness to a very ugly reality that is pervasive.

Again, I do believe the facade of legitimacy that Castro craves and I believe just got a helping hand—that is just not my view. The Washington Post and so many others have already opined on that in their editorials. This was not the time to take that view. There should have been an effort to say, human rights first, as you said, Mr. Antunez, then economic issues and other kinds of engagements.

I have seen one statement after another come out of Havana from high government officials that nothing is going to change. And, if anything, with the rearrests of at least five, maybe more, of the 53 and others who have been rounded up, which is the game that this regime plays in Cuba, just shows that they are intent on doubling down and making it even worse for the dissidents.

So thank you for, again, bearing witness to the truth and for exposing these crimes against humanity. And if you would like to make any final comment, Mr. Thale, starting with you and then finishing with Mr. Antunez.

Mr. THALE. Briefly. Only to say, Congressman Smith, obviously, I have the deepest respect for your commitment to human rights, particularly your focus on child trafficking and human trafficking issues.

Obviously, we differ about what is the best way to move forward in Cuba. And I am happy to continue that discussion.

The only very specific thing I would say on the human trafficking issue is that if you look at the U.N. human trafficking reports on Cuba, they are different than our Tier 3 listing. They are different because Cuba and the United States—Cuba has refused a dialogue with the United States about this issue. I believe that that is changing and there have been some discussions with the TIP unit, so——

Mr. SMITH. I am sorry.

Can I say, you know, the problem has been with some U.N. bureaucracies. I remember I held a hearing in this room on Elian Gonzalez. And Reverend Walker came and presented testimony and was waxing eloquent about how the child mortality rate is so low. And I had read the reports that came out of certain U.N. agencies that suggested that that was so.

And I asked him—because I know, one, as some of our witnesses have said earlier or as Ileana Ros-Lehtinen pointed out, trusting government officials to tender honest numbers, you know, if you believe that, I will sell you the Brooklyn Bridge. There is no reliability. There is no independent confirmation. There are no crosschecks or checks and balances whatsoever.

With that said, I also pointed out that Dr. Biscet, an OB/GYN Afro-Cuban, a great man, who has suffered horribly for his views on human rights, belief in human rights, he exposed eugenics policies in Cuba, where children who have disabilities are routinely killed through coercive abortion so that some of these kids never make it to birth because they have been killed by the state, and that is another crime against humanity.

It was called that at the Nuremberg War Crimes Tribunals, what the Nazis did to the Polish women and others. It is no less a crime against humanity today. Dr. Biscet suffered for that. So those numbers are very, very unreliable about child mortality and the like.

And as Ileana Ros-Lehtinen mentioned earlier, there is so much showcasing going on, but the ability to discern the real facts when others bear witness that that is not the case is very large.

Ms. Fonseca.

Ms. FONSECA. Yes. I have something to say. I remember that in 1990—I don't have a precise amount. I don't have a precise number. My youngest son was born prematurely. And where he was born, I saw several children die. However, I know that the hospital never reported those deaths. It was not known nationally or internationally.

I didn't like to listen to Fidel Castro's speeches, but sometimes I had to and I did because we need to know what the enemy says. And Fidel Castro is the enemy of Cuba.

I listened to the dictator's speech that year, and he said that—I don't know what the statistic was, but he referred to the child mortality rate in Cuba being very low. But having been pregnant and having had the difficult situation with my son, I had been in two hospitals. And I can assure you that many more children had died. But, also, I never received adequate medical assistance in order to help me in childbirth.

In Cuba, medicine and education are only good for those who are part of the regime or sympathize with the regime. That is my testimony with regards to the child mortality rate in Cuba and as to what kind of treatment a Cuban who dissents from the regime receives in schools and hospitals.

Mr. SMITH. Mr. Antunez.

Mr. GARCIA. I want to clearly establish something before we finish today. Maybe it hasn't been well understood, or maybe it is the regime's ability to spew false statistics sometimes confuses people.

I want to tell you that, in spite of the fact that there are some dissidents who do support Obama's policy toward Cuba—what I am referring to are the negotiations—I can tell you that it is a minority of dissidents.

I assure you that the majority of dissident leaders in Cuba, of opposition leaders in Cuba, oppose. And an example of this is the Forum for Rights and Freedoms, as well as the Agreement for Democracy in Cuba. Both of these initiatives have been signed by the most important leaders of the Cuban resistance.

There is one last thing which I also want to tell you because I know this is part of the permanent congressional record. And it is something that has worried me ever since I first heard it because I know that the victims don't have the possibility of speaking here. I ask those who are seeing me and those who are listening to me, all those who are well-intentioned are listening to this, I ask you to closely follow the repressive situation in Cuba right now. I want to call attention to how the Cuban National Civil Resistance Front, which consists of different organizations, is being repressed, not yesterday or not the day before yesterday, but right now, are being repressed because they are demanding freedom and democracy.

Finally, the struggle for Cuban freedom has cost a lot of pain, a lot of blood, a lot of dead, a lot of political prisoners, and that is why we can't allow that a maneuver by Raul Castro can result in an understanding with the U.S. Government that may contribute to oxygen being provided to this dictatorship and, therefore, to the continuity of the regime. I assure you that the permanency regime in power—I assure you that neo-Castroism can be worse than all these years we have suffered.

I want to thank you for this opportunity and especially Chairman Smith—and that the Cuban resistance, in spite of this agreement, which we consider to be immoral, in spite of the beatings, in spite of the imprisonment, in spite of the pain, the Cuban resistance will continue its struggle. We are not going to surrender our country's destiny to anyone because we are convinced that the principles and the destiny of a country should not be decided on a negotiating table. The destiny and the freedom of a country should not be decided at a negotiating table that the people have been excluded from.

I thank the U.S. Congress, I thank those in Cuba who are listening to us. I return to Cuba after this experience much more convinced of the path that we have taken. And I reiterate what is my slogan: I will not leave and I will not be quiet. Long live free Cuba.

Mr. SMITH. Thank you so much for that eloquent courage. Thank you all for your testimonies and leadership.

The hearing is adjourned.

[Whereupon, at 1:39 p.m., the subcommittee was adjourned.]

APPENDIX

MATERIAL SUBMITTED FOR THE RECORD

SUBCOMMITTEE HEARING NOTICE
COMMITTEE ON FOREIGN AFFAIRS
U.S. HOUSE OF REPRESENTATIVES
WASHINGTON, DC 20515-6128

Subcommittee on Africa, Global Health, Global Human Rights, and International Organizations
Christopher H. Smith (R-NJ), Chairman

February 5, 2015

TO: MEMBERS OF THE COMMITTEE ON FOREIGN AFFAIRS

You are respectfully requested to attend an OPEN hearing of the Committee on Foreign Affairs, to be held by the Subcommittee on Africa, Global Health, Global Human Rights, and International Organizations in Room 2172 of the Rayburn House Office Building (and available live on the Committee website at www.foreignaffairs.house.gov):

DATE: Thursday, February 5, 2015

TIME: 10:00 a.m.

SUBJECT: Human Rights in Cuba: A Squandered Opportunity

WITNESSES: Mr. Jorge Luis García Pérez
Secretary General
Cuban National Civic Resistance Front

Ms. Berta Soler Fernández
Leader
Ladies in White (*Damas de Blanco*)

Ms. Sara Martha Fonseca Quevedo
Member
Ladies in White (*Damas de Blanco*)

Mr. Geoff Thale
Program Director
Washington Office on Latin America

By Direction of the Chairman

The Committee on Foreign Affairs seeks to make its facilities accessible to persons with disabilities. If you are in need of special accommodations, please call 202/225-5021 at least four business days in advance of the event, whenever practicable. Questions with regard to special accommodations in general (including availability of Committee materials in alternative formats and assistive listening devices) may be directed to the Committee.

COMMITTEE ON FOREIGN AFFAIRS

MINUTES OF SUBCOMMITTEE ON _Africa, Global Health, Global Human Rights, and International Organizations_ HEARING

Day___ _Thursday___ Date___ _February 5, 2015___ Room _2172 Rayburn HOB_

Starting Time___ _10:03 a.m.___ Ending Time___ _1:39 p.m.___

Recesses |__1__| (_10:52_ to _11:53_) (____to ____) (____to ____) (____to ____) (____to ____) (____to ____)

Presiding Member(s)

Rep. Chris Smith

Check all of the following that apply:

Open Session ☑   Electronically Recorded (taped) ☑
Executive (closed) Session ☐   Stenographic Record ☑
Televised ☑

TITLE OF HEARING:

Human Rights in Cuba: A Squandered Opportunity

SUBCOMMITTEE MEMBERS PRESENT:

Rep. Karen Bass, Rep. David Cicilline, Rep. Tom Emmer, Rep. Curt Clawson

NON-SUBCOMMITTEE MEMBERS PRESENT: _(Mark with an * if they are not members of full committee.)_

Rep. Mario Diaz-Balart*, Rep. Ileana Ros-Lehtinen, Rep. Robert Pittenger*

HEARING WITNESSES: Same as meeting notice attached? Yes ☑ No ☐
(If "no", please list below and include title, agency, department, or organization.)

STATEMENTS FOR THE RECORD: _(List any statements submitted for the record.)_

Statement of Rep. Chris Smith, submitted by Rep. Chris Smith
Statement of Christopher J. Burgos of STFA, submitted by Rep. Chris Smith
Letter from the International Committee of Former Cuban Political Prisoners, submitted by Rep. Ileana Ros-Lehtinen
Agreement for Democracy in Cuba, submitted by Mr. Jorge Luis García Pérez
IAC precautionary measure for the Ladies in White, submitted by Ms. Berta Soler Fernández
Report by Cubalex, submitted by Ms. Berta Soler Fernández
Cuba Section of Trafficking in Persons Report, submitted by Rep. Chris Smith
Letter to President Obama from the STFA, submitted by Rep. Chris Smith
Statement on the human rights of all, submitted by Rep. Chris Smith

TIME SCHEDULED TO RECONVENE_____
or
TIME ADJOURNED___ _1:39 p.m.___

Gregory B. Simpkins
Subcommittee Staff Director

STATEMENT OF CHRISTOPHER J. BURGOS OF STFA SUBMITTED BY THE HONORABLE CHRISTOPHER H. SMITH, A REPRESENTATIVE IN CONGRESS FROM THE STATE OF NEW JERSEY, AND CHAIRMAN, SUBCOMMITTEE ON AFRICA, GLOBAL HEALTH, GLOBAL HUMAN RIGHTS, AND INTERNATIONAL ORGANIZATIONS

State Troopers Fraternal Association of New Jersey

STATEMENT

OF

CHRISTOPHER J BURGOS

PRESIDENT

STATE TROOPERS FRATERNAL ASSOCIATION OF NEW JERSEY, INC.

WRITTEN TESTIMONY

Subcommittee on Global Human Rights

House Foreign Affairs Committee

February 5th, 2015

Hearing on Human Rights Cuba

Chairman Smith and Members of the Committee,

Thank you for the invitation and the opportunity to submit my written testimony concerning Cuba relations and our concerns that Cuba harbors a convicted murderer of a New Jersey State Trooper, and other fugitives of the United States Justice System.

I am a twenty-nine year active veteran enlisted State Trooper with the New Jersey State Police (NJSP). I have been assigned to areas of patrol duties in many areas of our State, and have had the honor to work alongside other State Troopers who lived through the tragic events of May 2nd, 1973 on the New Jersey Turnpike. I have served as an elected Officer of my Association since 1999, and continue to serve as Association President since January 1st, 2012. In my capacity we have maintained a constant dialog on matters of mutual concern with our elected representatives at all levels. We have shared our experiences and concerns with State Troopers and Highway Patrolman all across the United States, as an active member of the National Troopers Coalition (NTC).

We at the State Troopers Fraternal Association of New Jersey (STFA NJ) represent the interests of almost 8,000 New Jersey State Troopers, going back to the founding of the NJSP in 1921, under the leadership and guidance of our first appointed NJSP Superintendent, Colonel H. Norman Schwarzkopf, a West Point graduate and U.S. Army Colonel at that time.

Our sphere of advocacy includes all active, retired, deceased, and the Sixty-Seven New Jersey State Troopers who paid the ultimate price of being killed in the line of duty. Part of our mission is to never forget and always remember the sacrifices given on behalf of our Great State and Nation.

The country of Cuba and the Castro regime have a long history of repression of human rights, despotism and brutality that has forced countless Cubans to seek refuge in the United States of America, in search of freedom and a better life. We believe that restoring diplomatic relations, without a clear commitment from the Cuban government of the steps they will take to reverse decades of human rights violations, will not result in a better and more just Cuba for its people.

At this juncture in re-establishing diplomatic relations, we believe there is an opportunity for Cuba and its government to show the American people and the citizens of the State of New Jersey it is serious about change.

The Cuban government has been providing safe haven to a Cop-Killer, convicted murderer Joanne Chesimard, a woman designated by the Federal Bureau of Investigation as a domestic terrorist, and the first woman ever placed on the FBI's "Most Wanted" Terrorist List.

In New Jersey, Joanne Chesimard is notorious for her role in the cold-blooded execution-style killing of New Jersey State Trooper Werner Foerster, Badge #2608, and seriously wounding New Jersey State Trooper James Harper, Badge #2108. On May 2nd, 1973, Chesimard, Clark Squire and Zayd Shakur were pulled over on the New Jersey Turnpike by Troopers Foerster and Harper for a motor vehicle violation.

Chesimard and both men in the car were armed with semi-automatic handguns, and possessed fictitious identification. During the motor vehicle stop, Chesimard initiated a gun battle, wounding Trooper James Harper.

In the shootout that followed, Chesimard's weapon was used to shoot Trooper Werner Foerster in the abdomen and then, as he lay incapacitated on the ground, Trooper Foerster's own weapon was used against him and he was brutally executed with two bullets to the head.

Chesimard was convicted in 1977 of first-degree murder and a number of other charges stemming from this brutally horrific incident and sentenced to life in prison. Chesimard, aided and abetted by armed accomplices, escaped from a New Jersey prison in 1979 and has been a fugitive from justice ever since. It is believed that she moved to Cuba in 1984 and has, since that time, lived freely there, attending government functions and being provided with housing, food, transportation and around the clock security by the Cuban government.

A long history of bipartisan support exists for the need to bring this convicted murderer back to the United States so she can be made to serve the prison time she was sentenced to, more than Thirty-Seven years ago. A few important points to consider:

- In 1998, the US. House of Representatives passed Concurrent Resolution 254 by a vote of 371-0 requesting that the Cuban government return Chesimard to the United States;

- In 1998, the US. Senate passed Concurrent Resolution 254 by unanimous consent requesting that the Cuban government return Chesimard to the United States;

- In 2005, the Department of Justice approved an increase In the reward for Chesimard's capture to $1 million; and

- In 2013, the Federal Bureau of Investigation placed Chesimard on its Most Wanted Terrorist List, designated her as a "domestic terrorist" and increased the reward for her capture to $2 million, which stands to this day

Cuba's provision of safe harbor to Chesimard by providing political asylum to a convicted cop killer, and her ability to elude justice, is an affront to every resident of our state, our country, and in particular, the men and women of the New Jersey State Police, who have tirelessly tried to bring this fugitive back to justice.

We urge you to demand and include the immediate return of Chesimard before any further consideration of restoration of diplomatic relations with the Cuban government. In addition, there certainly can be no review of Cuba's designation as a State Sponsor of Terrorism until Joanne Chesimard, a person designated by the FBI as a domestic terrorist, is returned to the United States of America.

If, as the White House asserts, Cuba is serious about embracing democratic principles then this action would be an essential first step. We ask to use this opportunity to engage with the Cuban government to get this resolved. We are shocked and very disappointed that returning a convicted killer of a State

Trooper was not already demanded and accomplished in the context of the steps announced by the White House regarding this despotic dictatorship.

In closing, the family of her victims, like so many of those who have, and continue to suffer under the Castro regime in Cuba, deserve this basic human decency before further steps towards Cuba are taken by the United States of America.

Thank you once again for allowing us to submit this written testimony to the Committee for consideration and inclusion in the record.

###

LETTER FROM THE INTERNATIONAL COMMITTEE OF FORMER CUBAN POLITICAL PRIS-
ONERS SUBMITTED BY THE HONORABLE ILEANA ROS-LEHTINEN, A REPRESENTATIVE
IN CONGRESS FROM THE STATE OF FLORIDA

Comité Internacional de Expresos Políticos Cubanos
COMISION POLITICA
508-43rd. St. Union City. NJ. 07087

Enero 15 del 2015.

De la Comisión Política del Comité Internacional de Expresos Políticos Cubanos.

Asunto: Las excarcelaciones en Cuba y los Presos Olvidados del Castrismo

El pasado 12 de Enero del 2015 el gobierno cubano notificó de la liberación de los presos políticos en lista provista por Estados Unidos y la Sección de Intereses del país norteamericano en la Habana anunció que pudo "verificar" las liberaciones. John Kerry, secretario de Estado de EE.UU. envió la relación de los 53 presos políticos excarcelados por Cuba al Senador demócrata Patrick Leahy, un simpatizante y mensajero " muy especial" para el régimen cubano.

La portavoz del Departamento de Estado, Marie Harf. declaró: "Damos la bienvenida a este paso positivo y aplaudimos la decisión del gobierno cubano de cumplir este compromiso".

Del análisis del referido listado podemos resumir:

- Siete habían sido excarcelados antes de la fecha de los acuerdos.

1.- Sonia Garro Alfonso.- **Excarcelada sin condena ni juicio después de 33 meses. Dic. 9. 2014**
2.- Ramón Alejandro Muñoz. **Excarcelado sin condena ni juicio después de 33 meses Dic. 9.2014**
3.- Eugenio Hernández Hdz. **Excarcelado sin condena ni juicio después de 33 meses. Dic. 9.2014**
4.- Vladimir Morera Bacallao.- **Excarcelado en Oct. 2014 por Huelga de Hambre**
5.- Marcelino Abreu Bonory.- **Excarcelado en Oct. 2014 por Huelga de Hambre**
6.- Eider Frometa Allen- **cumplió su condena en abril del 2014**
7.- Jorge Cervantes García.- **excarcelado en Agosto del 2014.**

Ni un nombre ni mención de los presos políticos, ya históricos, que guardan prisión en Cuba por razones de acciones contra el poder totalitario. De la omisión no sólo es responsable el Ejecutivo norteamericano sino sus "amigos" en Cuba y en el exilio que contribuyeron a la confección del listado.

Relación parcial no exenta de errores u omisiones:

	años cumplidos	desde	
Armando Sosa Fortuny.	18 + 20- 38	1994	
Humberto Eladio Real Suarez.	20	1994	
Miguel Díaz Bouza.	20	1994	
Santiago Padrón Quintero.	13	2001	
Máximo Praderas Valdés.	13	2001	
Francisco Chávez Abarca. **salvadoreño.**	4	2010	Entregado por Venezuela.
Ernesto Cruz León. **salvadoreño.**	17	1997	
Otto René Rodríguez Llorena. **salvadoreño.**	17	1997	
Leandro Cerezo Sirut.	7	2007	**Miembros del SMO que asaltaron base militar**
Karel de Miranda.	7	2007	" " " "
Yoan Torres Martínez	7	2007	" " " "
Alain Forbes Lamorú.	7	2007	" " " "
Pedro de la Caridad Álvarez Pedroso	23	1991	
Daniel Candelario Santovenia Fernández	23	1991	
Ernesto Borges Pérez.	16	1998	
Ihosvani Suris de la Torre.			Cadena perpetua.
Claro Fernando Alonso Hernández			Era oficial de inteligencia del Ministerio del Interior
Harold Alcalá Aramburu	13		2003 -Lancha de Regla "Baraguá" en causa donde fusilaron 3.

Maikel Delgado Aramburu	13	2003	"	"	"	"
Ramón Henri Grillo	13	2003	"	"	"	"
Wilmer Ledea Pérez	13	2003	"	"	"	"
Yoanny Thomas González.	13	2003	"	"	"	"
Miguel Álvarez.		Condenado a 25 años. Ex diplomático				
Lewis Arce Romero.		Cadena perpetua por intentar el desvío de un avión en Nueva G.				
Lázaro Ávila Sierra		Cadena perpetua por intentar el desvío de un avión en Nueva G.				
José Ángel Díaz Ortiz.		"		"	"	"
Francisco Reyes Rodríguez		"		"	"	"
Jorge Luis Pérez Puentes		"		"	"	"

Expresos políticos excarcelados con familiares en USA. que no le dan visa de entrada.

Jesús Manuel Rojas Pineda Díaz
Claro F. Alonso Hernández
Joel Cano Díaz
Tomas Ramos Rodríguez.
Rafael Ibarra

Con estas relaciones hacemos público y denunciamos el real alcance de lo que se ha anunciado como "un compromiso cumplido por parte de Cuba" y que en si esconde las verdaderas intenciones de las partes en cuanto a no reconocer el amplio espectro de los que han luchado para que el totalitarismo cubano no continúe perpetuándose en un suelo de vocación libertaria como el nuestro.

Cordialmente.

José A. Jiménez.
Guillermo Estévez.
Eduardo Ochoa.

16 (circled) Ya estában en la calle   16 + 37 = vr

COMISION CUBANA DE DERECHOS HUMANOS Y RECONCILIACION NACIONAL

ABREU BONORA	Marcelino	13-08-2012	Desacato y atentado	4 años	24-10-2014 Transferido a Trabajo Correccional sin Internamiento. (Detenido de nuevo y golpeado por la policia el 26-12-2014 y excarcelado el 06-01-2015 mediante Libertad Inmediata)	Detenido por expresar consignas contra el gobierno en una calle muy céntrica de La Habana. Miembro de la Unión Patriótica de Cuba (UNPACU).
GUERRA MARIN	Alcibiades	27-02-2014	Desacato a la figura de Fidel Castro.	1 año	30-12-2014 Cumplimiento de condena	Durante una protesta pública, expresó palabras consideradas ofensivas contra Fidel Castro.
CASTILLO GONZALEZ	Eliso	31/08/2012	Desacato y atentado	2 años	31-07-2014 Cumplimiento de condena	Activista de UNPACU. Condenado por expresarse contra el gobierno.
FROMETA ALLEN	Eider	20/02/2014	Daños a la propiedad del estado.	7 meses	04-07-2014 Cumplimiento de condena	Rompió el cristal de una de las puertas del auto de un oficial de la policía política.
CERVANTES GARCIA	Jorge	22/08/2012	Revocación de libertad condicional	3 años y 6 meses	06-08-2014 Cumplimiento de condena	Internado en prisión por sus actividades como dirigente de la Unión Patriótica de Cuba.
SANCHEZ PEREZ	César Andrés	03/07/2010	Desacato y atentado	6 años	29-01-2014 Libertad condicional	Fue condenado por expresar una broma durante un espectáculo público humorístico.
LEYVA DIAZ	José	24/04/2013	Presunto juego prohibido	1 año	24-04-2014 Cumplimiento de condena	Condenado por permitir que unos jóvenes realizaran juegos de mesa en su domicilio. Miembro del Movimiento Cubano Reflexión.
CARABALLO BETANCOURT	Madeline Lázara	01/10/2012	Instigación a delinquir, desorden público, desacato y resistencia.	4 años	25-04-2014 Libertad condicional	Condenada por oponerse al desalojo de varias familias, enfrentar a la policía y expresarse contra el gobierno.

COMISION CUBANA DE DERECHOS HUMANOS Y RECONCILIACION NACIONAL

La Habana, 14 de enero de 2015

RELACION DE PRESOS POLITICOS, DE LA LISTA DE 53, EXCARCELADOS A LO LARGO DE 2014

Registro legal solicitado al gobierno de Cuba desde 1987

1990 - Premio por la Libertad de Expresión de la Sociedad Interamericana de Prensa

1991 - Premio Internacional de Human Rights Watch

1996 - Premio de Derechos Humanos de la Republica Francesa

Apellidos	Nombres	Fecha de detención	Cargos	Condena	Fecha y condiciones de excarcelacion	Observaciones
RIVERA GUERRA	Niorvis	02-03-2012	Desorden público, lesiones, daños y otros actos	2 años y 6 meses	18-10-2014 Cumplimiento de condena	Detenido arbitrariamente por sus actividades opositoras como miembro de la Unión Patriótica de Cuba (UNPACU).
VAZQUEZ OSORIA	Juan Carlos	18-11-2012	Atentado.	2 años	10-12-2014 Cumplimiento de condena	Activista de la Unión Patriótica de Cuba. Encarcelado por participar en varias actividades pacíficas opositoras.
BUSTAMANTE RODRÍGUEZ	David	26-05-2014	Desórdenes públicos.	2 años	09-12-2014 Libertad condicional	Detenido y condenado por expresar consignas contra el gobierno.
GARRO ALFONSO	Sonia	18-03-2012	Desórdenes públicos y asesinato en grado de tentativa.	10 años (Petición fiscal)	09-12-2014 Excarcelada bajo condiciones no especificadas	Detenida violentamente por agentes policiales debido a sus actividades opositoras.
MUÑOZ GONZALEZ	Ramón Alejandro	18-03-2012	Desórdenes públicos y asesinato en grado de tentativa.	14 años (Petición fiscal)	09-12-2014 Excarcelado bajo condiciones no especificadas	Detenido violentamente por agentes policiales debido a sus actividades opositoras.
HERNÁNDEZ HERNÁNDEZ	Eugenio	18-03-2012	Desórdenes públicos y asesinato en grado de tentativa.	12 años (Petición fiscal)	09-12-2014 Excarcelado bajo condiciones no especificadas	Detenido violentamente por agentes policiales debido a sus actividades opositoras.
MICHELENA DIAZ	Yitliet	07-04-2014	Supuesto atentado	No condenada	07-11-2014 Excarcelada en el acto del juicio	Luego de ser detenida y esposada, fue agredida por una agente parapolicial
MORERA BACALLAO	Vladimir	04-09-2013	Desórdenes públicos, atentado, desacato y daños.	8 años	27-09-2014 Licencia Extra Penal	Activista sindical. Participó en un enfrentamiento verbal contra agentes parapoliciales.

(37)

COMISION CUBANA DE DERECHOS HUMANOS Y RECONCILIACION NACIONAL

EXCARCELADOS LOS DIAS 7 Y 8 DE ENERO QUE FORMAN PARTE DE LA LISTA DE 53 PRESOS POLITICOS

Registro legal solicitado al gobierno de Cuba desde 1987

1990 - Premio por la Libertad de Expresión de la Sociedad Interamericana de Prensa

1991 - Premio Internacional de Human Rights Watch.

1996 - Premio de Derechos Humanos de la Republica Francesa

APELLIDOS	NOMBRES	DETENCION	CARGOS	CONDENA	FECHA Y CONDICIONES DE EXCARCELACION	OBSERVACIONES
PLANA ROBERT	Emilio	23-09-2012	Peligrosidad social Pre-delictiva.	3 años y 6 meses	08-01-2015 Suspensión de Medida de Seguridad	Condenado arbitrariamente por su destacada actividad como miembro de la Unión Patriótica de Cuba (UNPACU)
ARCE SARMIENTO	Yojames	13-05-2014	Atentado	3 años	08-01-2015 Licencia Extra Penal	Víctima de un "acto de repudio" por expresarse contra el gobierno. Activista de la UNPACU.
RODRÍGUEZ NAVARRO	José Manuel	03-10-2013	Peligrosidad Social Pre-delictiva	4 años	08-01-2015 Suspensión de Medida de Seguridad	Detenido arbitrariamente bajo la sospecha de que había escrito letreros contra el gobierno. Activista de la UNPACU.
PILOTO BARCELÓ	David	21-01-2011	Desacato y desórdenes públicos	5 años	08-01-2015 Libertad Condicional	Opositor activo, detenido por distribuir proclamas frente al Consejo de Estado.
MENDOZA COBAS	Yordenis	20-03-2014	Atentado y Desobediencia	3 años	08-01-2015 Licencia Extra Penal	Sostuvo una discusión con un agente policial. Activista de la UNPACU.
OTERO RODRÍGUEZ	Alexander	26-03-2013	Atentado	5 años	08-01-2015 Libertad Condicional	Activista de la Unión Patriótica de Cuba. Fue víctima de un "acto de repudio".
VARGAS MARTIN	Alexeis	27-11-2012	Desacato, resistencia, desorden público y amenazas.	4 años	08-01-2015 Libertad Condicional	Activista de la Unión Patriótica de Cuba. Víctima de un "acto de repudio" durante el cual se enfrentó a la policía política.
VEGA SANTISTEBAN	Julio César	18-01-2013	Revocación por un supuesto atentado.	4 años	08-01-2015 Libertad Condicional	Encarcelado por sus múltiples actividades como miembro de la UNPACU.
LABRADOR DÍAZ	Luis Enrique	21-01-2011	Desacato y desórdenes públicos	5 años	08-01-2015 Libertad Condicional	Opositor activo, detenido por distribuir proclamas frente al Consejo de Estado.
RAMÍREZ CALDERÓN	Jorge	18-10-2013	Desórdenes públicos, atentado y desacato.	4 años	08-01-2015 Licencia Extra Penal	Activista sindical. Participó en un enfrentamiento verbal contra agentes parapoliciales.

COMISION CUBANA DE DERECHOS HUMANOS Y RECONCILIACION NACIONAL

REMÓN ARZUAGA	Ángel Yunier	26-03-2013	Atentado	6 años	08-01-2015 Licencia Extra Penal	Activista de la Unión Patriótica de Cuba. Fue víctima de un "acto de repudio".
REYES RABANAL	Rolando	08-05-2014	Pendiente	Pendiente	08-01-2015 Cambio de Medida Cautelar	Detenido por participar en una manifestación pacífica en una calle céntrica de La Habana.
MAINET VILLALÓN	Rubertandis	26-08-2013	Desacato y atentado	5 años	08-01-2015 Licencia Extra Penal	Activista de la Unión Patriótica de Cuba. Encarcelado por realizar numerosas actividades pacíficas.
GUERRA HASTIE	Miguel	04-04-2013	Atentado	3 años	08-01-2015 Licencia Extra Penal	Activista de la Unión Patriótica de Cuba. Fue "víctima de un acto de repudio".
RIVEAUX NOA	Aracelio	27-11-2012	Desacato, resistencia, desorden público y amenaza	2 años y 6 meses	08-01-2015 Libertad Condicional	Activista de la Unión Patriótica de Cuba. Víctima de un "acto de repudio".
QUESADA CHAVECO	Daniel Enrique	15-08-2013	Atentado	2 años	08-01-2015 Licencia Extra Penal	Activista de la Unión Patriótica de Cuba. Encarcelado y condenado de manera arbitraria.
FIGUEREDO CASTELLÓN	Angel	26-05-2014	Pendiente	Pendiente	08-01-2015 Cambio de Medida Cautelar	Participó en una protesta pacífica incluyendo expresiones verbales contra el gobierno.
GALLARDO SALAZAR	Haydée	26-05-2014	Pendiente	Pendiente	08-01-2015 Libertad inmediata	Participó en una protesta pacífica incluyendo expresiones verbales contra el gobierno.
TAMAYO GUERRA	Ernesto	15-05-2014	Pendiente	Pendiente	08-01-2015 Cambio de Medida Cautelar	Detenido por participar en una manifestación pacífica en una calle céntrica de La Habana.
TAMAYO FRIAS	Miguel Ángel	13-06-2014	Pendiente	Pendiente	08-01-2015 Cambio de Medida Cautelar	Detenido por participar en una manifestación pacífica en una calle céntrica de La Habana.
ORTIZ SUÁREZ	Vladimir	13-06-2014	Pendiente	Pendiente	08-01-2015 Cambio de Medida Cautelar	Detenido por participar en una manifestación pacífica en una calle céntrica de La Habana.
FERNÁNDEZ DEPESTRE	Iván	30-07-2013	Peligrosidad Social Pre-Delictiva	3 años	08-01-2015 Suspensión de Medida de Seguridad	Miembro del Movimiento de Resistencia Cívica. Detenido por sospecharse que había escrito letreros antigubernamentales.
ALMEIDA PÉREZ	Aroy	05-09-2013	Desórdenes públicos.	2 años	08-01-2015 Licencia Extra Penal	Fue detenido junto a otro opositor cuando se dirigía a un video-debate.

COMISION CUBANA DE DERECHOS HUMANOS Y RECONCILIACION NACIONAL

ASCENCIO LÓPEZ	José Lino	05-09-2013	Desórdenes públicos.	3 años y 6 meses	08-01-2015 Licencia Extra Penal	Fue detenido junto a otro opositor cuando se dirigía a un video-debate.
PARADA MILÁN	Wilberto	30-03-2013	Atentado, desacato y resistencia.	4 años	08-01-2015 Licencia Extra Penal	Protestó por una arbitrariedad policial. Activista de la Unión Patriótica de Cuba.
HERNÁNDEZ BARRIOS	Roberto	30-3-2013	Desacato, atentado y resistencia	5 años	08-01-2015 Licencia Extra Penal	Protestó por una arbitrariedad policial... Activista de la Unión Patriótica de Cuba.
PAUMIER RAMÍREZ	Leonardo	13-06-2014	Pendiente	Pendiente	08-01-2015 Cambio de Medida Cautelar	Detenido por participar en una manifestación pacífica en una calle céntrica de La Habana.
MULET LEVIS	Reiner	09-04-2013	Daños a la propiedad del Estado	3 años	08-01-2015 Libertad Condicional	Pintó letreros contra el gobierno en lugares públicos.
ULLOA GINARD	Miguel Alberto	10-04-2013	Daños a la propiedad del Estado	2 años	08-01-2015 Libertad Condicional	Pintó letreros contra el gobierno en lugares públicos.
VARGAS MARTÍN	Bianko	02-12-2012	Desacato, Resistencia, Desorden Público y Amenaza	2 años y 6 meses	07-01-2015 Libertad Condicional	Activista de la Unión Patriótica de Cuba. Víctima de un "acto de repudio".
VARGAS MARTÍN	Diango	02-12-2012	Desacato, Resistencia, Desorden Público y Amenaza	2 años y 6 meses	07-01-2015 Libertad Condicional	Activista de la Unión Patriótica de Cuba. Víctima de un "acto de repudio".
FIGUEROLA MIRANDA	Enrique	28-07-2012	Atentado	3 años	07-01-2015 Libertad Condicional	Detenido por su destacado activismo en la Unión Patriótica de Cuba.
RIVERY GASCÓN	Ernesto Roberto	27-11-2012	Desacato, resistencia, desorden público y amenazas.	3 años	07-01-2015 Libertad Condicional	Activista de la Unión Patriótica de Cuba. Víctima de un "acto de repudio".
ROMERO HURTADO	Lázaro	27-11-2012	Desacato, resistencia, desorden público y amenazas	5 años	07-01-2015 Libertad Condicional	Activista de la Unión Patriótica de Cuba. Víctima de un "acto de repudio".
FERNÁNDEZ RICO	Alexander Roberto	17-04-2012	Desacato	3 años	08-01-2015 Libertad Condicional	Detenido y condenado por protestar y decir consignas contra el gobierno.
FIGUEROA ALVAREZ	Carlos Manuel	15-05-2013	Atentado	Pendiente	08-01-2015 Libertad Condicional	Opositor activo. Golpeado brutalmente y detenido por agentes policiales.
MEJÍAS ZULUETA	Sandalio	16-05-2014	Peligrosidad Social Pre- Delictiva.	3 años	08-01-2015 Suspensión de Medida de Seguridad	Miembro del opositor Partido Liberal. Condenado por sus actividades contestatarias.

MATERIAL SUBMITTED FOR THE RECORD BY MR. JORGE LUIS GARCÍA PÉREZ,
SECRETARY GENERAL, CUBAN NATIONAL CIVIC RESISTANCE FRONT

Agreement for Democracy in Cuba

We, Cubans conscious of the need for transcendental change in the political, social and economic structures of our country, gather, beyond our diverse strategies for liberation, to affirm before our people and the international community the essential postulates that substantiate the democratic alternative to the despotism which currently prevails in our homeland.

We affirm that the Cuban nation is one, within the national territory and in diaspora. We believe that all Cubans have the right to be equal before the law and the nation, with full dignity that cannot be subject to any discrimination. We likewise understand that the present regime has shown itself incapable of assuring liberty and justice and of promoting well-being and human solidarity in our homeland. Due to this, from this point forward, we establish, through a great national consensus and as a clear alternative to the current oppression, this:

Agreement for Democracy in Cuba

We recognize as the fundamental principle of the new Republic that Cuba is one and independent, whose sovereignty resides in the people and functions through the effective exercise of representative multi-party democracy, which is the government of the majority with absolute respect for the minority.

All governments must respect the sovereignty of the people, therefore, at the end of the current tyrannical regime, the provisional or transition government shall be obligated to return sovereignty to the people by way of the following measures:

(1) Guarantee the people's participation in the decisions of the nation through the exercise of universal, direct, and secret voting to elect its representatives, and the right to seek public office.

(2) Immediately issue a general amnesty for the liberation of all political prisoners, including those who have been sentenced for fictitious common crimes, and cancel the pending political cases against Cubans in exile, so as to facilitate their return to the homeland and their reintegration into the national society.

(3) Organize an independent, impartial, and professional judiciary.

(4) Recognize and protect the freedom of expression, of the press, of association, of assembly, of peaceful demonstration, profession, and religion.

(5) Protect the Cuban people from arbitrary expulsion from their homes as well as against all forms of detention, search, confiscation or arbitrary aggression, and from violation of their correspondence, documents and other communications, and defend all Cubans' rights to privacy and honor.

(6) Immediately legalize all political parties and other organizations and activities of civil society.

(7) Refer to the Constitution of 1940, when applicable, during the transition period and convoke free elections with the supervision of international organizations within a time period not greater than one year, for a Constituent Congress which will establish a Constitution and which, during its existence, shall have authority to legislate as well as to oversee the executive. Having thus achieved democratic legitimacy, it shall call general elections in accordance with the provisions of the Constitution.

(8) Recognize and protect the freedom of economic activity; the right to private property; the right to unionize, to bargain collectively and to strike; the Cuban people's right to genuine participation in their economic development; access to public health and education, and initiate the reestablishment of civic values in education.

(9) Take immediate steps to protect Cuba's environmental security and protect and rescue the national patrimony.

(10) Propitiate and guarantee the professionalism and political neutrality of the Armed Forces and create forces of public order whose rules of conduct shall adjust to the principles of this Agreement.

Cuba shall resurrect from its own ashes, but it is the sacred obligation of all Cubans - both within the oppressed island and in diaspora - to place our hands on the plough without looking backwards but rather into the deepest part of our hearts, to convert those ashes into fertile seeds of love and creation. Now, as 100 years ago, our national aspiration remains the construction of a Republic based on the formula of triumphant love:

WITH ALL AND FOR THE GOOD FOR ALL

Signed February 20, 1998   Reaffirmed: August 31; 2007
La Habana, Cuba   Lubin, Poland
Miami, Florida

**INTER-AMERICAN COMMISSION ON HUMAN RIGHTS
RESOLUTION N. 6/2013**

PRECAUTIONARY MEASURE No. 264-13
Topic Ladies in White regarding the Republic of Cuba[1]
October 28, 2013

I. INTRODUCTION

1. On June 13, 2013, the Inter-American Commission on Human Rights (hereinafter "the Inter-American Commission", "the Commission" or "IACHR") received a request for precautionary measures submitted by the "Cubalex Legal Information Center" (hereinafter "the petitioners"), seeking that the Republic of Cuba (hereinafter "Cuba" or "the State") protect the life and physical integrity of the members of the organization "Ladies in White" (hereinafter "the proposed beneficiaries" or "the organization"). According to the request, due to a series of peaceful demonstrations that the proposed beneficiaries held for the purpose of exposing the situation of suspected political dissidents in Cuba, their members are subjected to threats, harassment and violence against them, in retaliation for their activities.

2. After requesting additional information from the petitioners, they provided information on September 17 and 26, 2013.

3. After analyzing the factual and legal arguments presented by the petitioners, the Commission considers that the information presented shows *prima facie* that the members of the "Ladies in White" organization are in a serious and urgent situation, as their lives and physical integrity are threatened and at severe risk. Consequently, in accordance with Article 25 of its Rules of Procedure, the Commission requests that the Government of Cuba: a) adopt the necessary measures to guarantee the life and physical integrity of the members of the "Ladies in White" organization; b) agree on the measures to be adopted with the beneficiaries and their representatives; and c) report on the actions taken to investigate the facts that gave rise to the precautionary measures, in order to prevent future incidents.

II. SUMMARY OF ALLEGATIONS BY THE PETITIONERS

4. According to the request and subsequent communications presented by the petitioners, the "Ladies in White" is an organization of women who hold peaceful gatherings, in order to protest and expose the human rights situation that their families are facing, as alleged political dissidents in Cuba. The petitioners claim that their members attend Mass every Sunday in different Catholic churches, dressed in white and usually carry pictures of their relatives and flowers. After church services, they march silently through various streets throughout various locations in Cuba. In the request for precautionary measures, the following allegations are made:

a) There is a context of violent repression against the "Ladies in White". Specifically, they claim that the marches and rallies of the proposed beneficiaries are known as "counterrevolutionary demonstrations" by the State authorities, who make threats, and perpetrate acts of harassment and violence against them, in order to prevent them from executing their activities. According to the petitioners, the State authorities operate, together with civil society groups known as "repudiation meetings" and "Rapid Response Brigades" (hereinafter BRR). These groups are "formed institutionally, in centers of work, study and neighborhoods, through social organizations", who have

---

[1] On January 31st, 1962, the Government of Cuba was excluded from its participation in the inter-American system by Resolution VI adopted in the Eighth Meeting of Consultation of Ministers of Foreign Affairs, held in Punta del Este (Uruguay). On June 3, 2009, during its Thirty-Ninth Ordinary Session Period held in Honduras, the General Assembly of the Organization of American States (OAS) revoked the Resolution VI adopted in the Eighth Meeting of Consultation of Ministers of Foreign Affairs and determined that "the participation of the Republic of Cuba in the OAS will be the result of a process of dialogue initiated at the request of the Government of the Republic of Cuba and in accordance with the practices, purposes and principles of the OAS."

the mission of "rejecting anti-revolutionary movements and disturbances using simple weapons: sticks, steel bars and cables." The petitioners point out that the State authorities presumably summon these groups outside the homes of the proposed beneficiaries, seeking to prevent them from attending Mass. The "Ladies in White" that manage to leave their homes and attend Mass, are detained afterwards, with an excessive use of force by State security officers and by the National Revolutionary Police.

b) The detentions are imposed for short periods –of between 4 and 12 hours on average. In the detention centers, "the officers use violence, insults and sexual offenses, as a means of repression." According to the petitioners, "they are locked away in dungeons, in unsanitary conditions, [...] even sharing cells with men." In some situations, they are "forced to undress or are stripped naked, [...] to squat in order to check if they have items hidden in their genitals". They claim that, in some cases, objects were introduced into the vagina of one of the detainees, "under the justification of searching for recording devices". They assert that, on several occasions, officers made several comments and jokes about their genitals and underwear, among other things. During detention, they state that they are not allowed to make phone calls, drink water or eat. After the detentions, the "Ladies in White" are released and "left miles away from their homes, in unpopulated areas and away from public transport".

c) In the past months the repression against the "Ladies in White" has increased, mainly in the towns of Matanzas, Cardenas and Colón. On July 7, 2013, the parish priest of the Church of "San José", in the town of Colón, prevented members of the BRR from attacking seven "Ladies in White". On July 14, 2013, after Mass, "a meeting of repudiation" beat several members of the organization, including Mrs. Sonia Alvarez Campillo, who suffered from a fracture of her left arm. On July 21, 2013, after attending Mass at the Church of the "Sacred Heart", Municipality of Cárdenas, 14 "Ladies in White" were allegedly violently repressed by State authorities: in particular, Leticia Ramos who was hit in her right eye and on her head, for which she was diagnosed with head trauma. On August 4, 2013, there were new detentions of the proposed beneficiaries in the provinces of Holguín, Pinar del Río, Havana and Guantánamo. On August 11, 2013, when leaving the Church of the "Holy Conception", Municipality of Cárdenas, eleven "Ladies in White" were arrested and beaten. In the case of Elizabeth Pacheco Lamas, she was beaten and dragged, leaving her with "excoriation on her knees".

d) During September 2013, the risk faced by the members of the "Ladies in White" increased and there were further detentions. On September 22, 2013, one detention in the province of Pinar del Río, five in Havana, two in Mayabeque, 19 in Matanzas, five in Villa Clara and three in Guantánamo were reported. On September 23, 2013, 13 arrests took place in Havana to prevent them from participating in the "literary tea" (book club) at the organization headquarters. On September 24, 2013, there were reports of two new arrests in Havana, in order to prevent them from participating in the commemoration of the "Las Mercedes Day". Among the testimonies presented, the following may be highlighted: i) Katyuska Rodríguez Rivas, who was arrested on September 22, 2013, after Mass by members of the BRR, who beat her with an umbrella, while officials grabbed her by her arms; ii) Marielis Díaz Torres, when leaving her home at 8:00 am on September 22, 2013, to head to Mass at the Church of the "Cathedral", was intercepted by a security officer from the State. This person presumably detained her in an official woodwork shop until 11:00 am. They claim that the officer that held her reportedly warned her "that every Sunday would be the same."

e) The petitioners allege that despite the acts of violence against them, the State ensures impunity for the perpetrators. In the words of the petitioners, "the personal safety and physical integrity of the group 'Ladies in White' is at risk and their lives are in danger, due to the acts of violence unleashed on them by [...] State officials [...], in order to prevent them from exercising their religious freedom, freedom of speech, association, assembly and expression."

III. ANALYSIS OF THE ELEMENTS OF GRAVITY, URGENCY AND IRREPARABILITY

5. The mechanism of precautionary measures is a part of the Commission's function of overseeing Member State compliance with the human rights obligations set forth in Article 106 of the Charter of the Organization of American States. These general oversight functions are set forth in Article 41 (b) of the American Convention on Human Rights, and Article 18 of the Commission's Statute. The mechanism of precautionary measures is set out in

Article 25 of the Commission's Rules of Procedure. According to this Article, the Commission issues precautionary measures in situations that are serious and urgent, and where such measures are necessary to prevent irreparable harm to persons.

6. The Inter-American Commission and the Inter-American Court of Human Rights have repeatedly established that precautionary and provisional measures have a dual nature, precautionary and protective. Regarding their protective nature, the measures seek to avoid irreparable harm and preserve the exercise of human rights. Regarding their precautionary nature, the measures have the purpose of preserving a legal situation being considered by the IACHR. Their precautionary nature aims to preserve those rights at risk until the petition in the Inter-American system is resolved. Its object and purpose are to ensure the integrity and effectiveness of the decision on the merits and, thus, avoid infringement of the rights at issue, a situation that may adversely affect the useful purpose (*effet utile*) of the final decision. In this regard, precautionary measures or provisional measures thus enable the State concerned to fulfill the final decision and, if necessary, to comply with the reparations ordered. As such, for the purposes of making a decision, and in accordance with Article 25.2 of its Rules of Procedure, the Commission considers that:

a. "serious situation" refers to a grave impact that an action or omission can have on a protected right or on the eventual effect of a pending decision in a case or petition before the organs of the Inter-American system;
b. "urgent situation" refers to risk or threat that is imminent and can materialize, thus requiring immediate preventive or protective action; and
c. "irreparable harm" refers to injury to rights which, due to their nature, would not be susceptible to reparation, restoration or adequate compensation.

7. In the present situation, the Commission considers that the requirement of gravity is met, in view of the allegations of threats, acts of intimidation, and violence and a series of short-term detentions –including episodes in which they were allegedly forced, *inter alia*, to undress and undergo genital checks– against the "Ladies in White". Specifically, the information suggests that the situation arises as a form of retaliation and intimidation against them, due to their peaceful protests in relation to the situation of their families, as political dissidents in Cuba.

8. In the context of the analysis of this requirement, the Commission notes that the information provided by the petitioners is consistent with the general information that the Commission has received on the hostile environment against members of the said organization, which manifests itself in constant physical attacks against them and a number of arbitrary short-term detentions. These circumstances have led the Commission to express concern in different Annual Reports from several years. In this regard, in Chapter IV of the Annual Report[2] of 2012, about Cuba, the Commission noted an apparent exacerbation of the situation of the "Ladies in White", in the context of the visit of Pope Benedict XVI to Cuba. In particular, concerning the constant harassment and detention against them, as a mechanism to limit or restrict their right of assembly or to self expression.

9. Similarly, the United Nations System has been continuously monitoring the situation of the "Ladies in White", through different mechanisms and special procedures. In this regard, during 2012, the Special Rapporteurs on the promotion and protection of the right to freedom of opinion and expression; on the rights to freedom of peaceful assembly and of association; on the freedom of religion or belief; and Special Rapporteur on Human Rights Defenders, provided particular follow-up to information received on the arbitrary detention, harassment and violation of the right of assembly of the members of the "Ladies in White"[3]. In particular, the Rapporteurs

---

[2] See: IACHR. Chapter IV – Cuba in the IACHR 2012 Annual Report; Chapter IV - Cuba in the IACHR 2011 Annual Report; Chapter IV – Cuba in the IACHR 2010 Annual Report; Chapter IV – Cuba in the IACHR 2009 Annual Report; Chapter IV – Cuba in the IACHR 2008 Annual Report; among others.

[3] See: UN. Communications sent, in the framework of the Special Procedures of the Human Rights Council, by the Special Rapporteur on the promotion and protection of the right to freedom of opinion and expression; Special Rapporteur on the right of association and pacific assembly; Special Rapporteur on freedom of religion or creed; and Special Rapporteur on the situation of human rights defenders," dated March 21, 2012 and October 9, 2012.

mentioned that they had "urge[d] the Government [...] to take all necessary measures to protect the rights and freedoms of members of the 'Ladies in White' organization and investigate, prosecute and impose appropriate sanctions on any person responsible for the violations against them."[4]

10. Taking into consideration the above-mentioned background and characteristics of the present situation, the Commission considers *prima facie* that the right to life and physical integrity of the members of the "Ladies in White" are at risk, due to their activities.

11. Regarding the requirement of urgency, the Commission considers that it is satisfied, as the alleged acts of violence and presumably repeated detentions have consistently increased over time, without protective measures being made available on behalf of the "Ladies in White". In these circumstances, the Commission considers that various factors converge - the status of a specific group of female human rights defenders, who are constantly under the State's custody in the context of short-term detentions. The situation requires the immediate adoption of special protection measures, in order to avert the various risk scenarios to which they are constantly exposed and allow them to carry out their activities safely.

12. On the requirement of irreparability, the Commission believes that it has been met, to the extent that the possible risk to the right to life and physical integrity embodies the highest situation of irreparability.

13. Under Article 25.5, the Commission normally requests information from the State before taking a decision on request for precautionary measures, except in matters as in the present situation where the immediacy of the potential harm does not allow delays.

14. The Commission wishes to reaffirm the importance of the work of human rights defenders in the region. In this regard, the Commission has consistently indicated the importance of the work carried out by persons engaged in the promotion, monitoring and advocacy of human rights and the organizations to which many of them are affiliated. In this regard, the OAS General Assembly in its resolution AG/RES 2579 (XL-0/10) recognized the work that female human rights defenders are doing within the region and resolved to recognize that, in view of their gender-specific role and their needs and the particular risks they face by virtue of the discrimination they have traditionally suffered, women human rights defenders should be accorded special attention to ensure that they are fully protected and are effective in carrying out their important activities. In these circumstances, the Commission considers that acts of violence and other attacks against human rights defenders not only affect the guarantees of any human being, but they undermine their fundamental role in society and render all those that they represent, helpless.

IV. BENEFICIARIES

15. The request was submitted on behalf of the members of the "Ladies in White", who represent approximately 237 persons, fully identified in the lists submitted by the petitioners and who may be identifiable due to their affiliation with the organization.

V. DECISION

16. In view of the above-mentioned information, the Commission considers that this matter *prima facie* meets the requirements of gravity, urgency and irreparable harm contained in Article 25 of its Rules of Procedure. Consequently, the Commission requests that the Government of Cuba:

> a) adopt all necessary measures to protect the life and physical integrity of the members of the "Ladies in White" organization;

---

[4] Ibid.

b) agree on the measures to be adopted with the beneficiaries and their representatives; and,

c) report on the actions taken to investigate the facts that gave rise to the precautionary measures, in order to prevent future incidents.

17. The Commission also requests the Government of Cuba to inform, within 15 days from the date of the issuance of this resolution, on the adoption of the required precautionary measures and to update said information on an ongoing basis.

18. The Commission emphasizes that, according to article 25 (8) of its Rules of Procedure, the granting of this precautionary measure and its adoption by the State shall not constitute a pre-judgment on any possible violation of the rights protected in the American Declaration and other applicable instruments.

19. The Commission orders the Secretariat of the Inter-American Commission to notify the State of Cuba and the applicants of this resolution.

20. Approved on the 28th day of October, 2013, by: José Orozco, President; Tracy Robinson, First Vice President; Rosa María Ortiz, Second Vice President; Commissioners Felipe González, Dinah Shelton and Rodrigo Escobar Gil.

centre de información legal

Cuba: Situación de derechos humanos de las "Damas de Blanco Laura Pollán"

29/10/2013

En el seno de las Naciones Unidas y de la Organización de Estado Americanos, se ha reconocido la legitimidad y el papel decisivo que desempeñan las y los defensores de los derechos humanos, así como la necesidad de realizar esfuerzos especiales para protegerlos.

Situación de derechos humanos de las "Damas de Blanco" en Cuba

Contenido

SITUACIÓN DE DERECHOS HUMANOS DE LAS "DAMAS DE BLANCO" EN CUBA

Las Damas de Blanco como defensoras de los Derechos Humanos

En marzo de 2003 el gobierno cubano arrestó y enjuició a 75 disidentes, defensores de los derechos humanos. Los hechos se conocieron como la Primavera Negra de Cuba. Desde entonces madres, hijas, hermanas y esposas de estos defensores vestidas de blanco, los domingos asisten a misa en diferentes Iglesias Católicas a lo largo de la isla. Después de terminar la ceremonia religiosa, marchan en silencio con flores en las manos. Durante una década han visualizado la situación de injusticia e impunidad dentro de la isla, exponiéndose a amenazas y acosos, restricciones de su libertad de asociación, expresión y reunión pacífica, hechos que han repercutido negativamente en su labor y seguridad. No obstante, desde noviembre de 2011, el movimiento se extendió a casi toda la isla, con una cifra de más de 300 mujeres en la actualidad.

Las Damas de Blanco son un grupo de mujeres que abogan por la liberación de los presos políticos y el respeto de los derechos humanos dentro de la Isla, y como defensoras, realizan protestas pacíficas vinculadas a demandas de reformas democráticas y a la promoción de los derechos civiles y políticos. Como Asociación, no posee personalidad jurídica, sin embargo, no es necesario que el colectivo esté reconocido por el Estado como una ONG, debido a que el derecho a participar en actividades pacíficas puede ser ejercido de forma individual o en asociación.

Se reúnen en una residencia particular, que constituye su sede, realizan marchas, con el objetivo de promover y proteger los derechos humanos de manera pacífica, respetando los principios de universalidad y no violencia.

Acusadas de representar intereses extranjeros, son estigmatizadas políticamente como "enemigas del Estado", por parte de las autoridades y de los medios de comunicación propiedad del Estado, para deslegitimar el trabajo que realizan, situación que aumenta su vulnerabilidad. Los medios de comunicación participan activamente en las violaciones cometidas en contra de ellas, en particular, en relación con violaciones de su derecho a la privacidad. Las campañas de denigración en la prensa y la televisión propiedad estatal, sin derecho a réplica, hacen que sean percibidas como "alborotadoras" y por lo tanto se legitimen los ataques en su contra.

Actualmente dentro del sistema legal nacional, no existe ninguna norma que les ofrezca protección eficaz, al reaccionar u oponerse, por medios pacíficos, a actividades, actos u omisiones, imputables al Estado y que causan violaciones de los derechos humanos y las libertades fundamentales. No disfrutan de un

entorno seguro, porque el Estado incumple su obligación de procesar y castigar a los culpables, favoreciendo la impunidad.

Situación de las defensoras dentro de Cuba:

Restricciones al derecho de protesta en el sistema legal cubano

El derecho a la protesta es un elemento fundamental del derecho de participación política y social en toda estructura democrática y los Estados tienen la obligación de adoptar medidas deliberadas, concretas y selectivas para promover, mantener y fortalecer el pluralismo, la tolerancia y una actitud abierta con respecto a la disensión en la sociedad.

En el sistema legal cubano existen leyes incompatibles con las normas internacionales, que son utilizadas por el gobierno para legitimar las violaciones de los derechos humanos y dificultar enormemente la labor de las defensoras. Es constante la violación de sus derechos relativos a la libertad de opinión y de expresión, al acceso a la información, al acceso a los recursos, y a las libertades de asociación (incluyendo el registro) y reunión pacífica y de locomoción.

A- El derecho a la participación en manifestaciones públicas no encuentra reconocimiento constitucional ni desarrollo legal. El Código Penal, al proteger los derechos individuales[1], incluye el derecho de manifestación y sanciona al que, con infracción de las disposiciones legales, impida la celebración de una reunión o manifestación lícita o que una persona concurra a ellas. Si el delito se comete por un funcionario público, con abuso de su cargo, la pena se duplica. Sin embargo, el propio cuerpo legal[2] considera que, comete un delito que atenta contra el orden público, quienes participen en reuniones o manifestaciones celebradas con infracción de las disposiciones, que regulan el ejercicio de ese derecho. Disposiciones que no existen. Triplica la sanción para los organizadores de las mismas. No existe procedimiento para notificar o solicitar autorización para realizar una protesta, ni recursos legales para apelar las decisiones denegatorias. No obstante, son frecuentes los desfiles por céntricas avenidas, convocadas y organizadas por el propio gobierno, con un marcado carácter político-ideológico. Las restricciones impuestas por el estado a este derecho, no están provistas en una ley.

B- En el país no existe ninguna organización para promover y proteger los derechos humanos y la mayoría de las Organizaciones No Gubernamentales existentes, son establecidas por el gobierno y defienden sus intereses, sin contar que la mayoría de los ciudadanos no

---

[1] Artículo 292 Código Penal
[2] Artículo 209 Código Penal

son consultados a la hora de ser inscritos en las mismas[3]. Estas organizaciones llevan un control de la vida privada de los ciudadanos y emiten valoraciones que inciden en su vida social, laboral y económica[4].

C- Por su parte, la ley de Asociaciones impone fuertes restricciones para el registro, financiación, gestión y funcionamiento de las Organizaciones No Gubernamentales en el sistema legal cubano, con la intención de controlar sus actividades y filtrar a los grupos que critican las políticas del gobierno[5].

D- El gobierno sólo se permite que las agrupaciones de individuos realicen actividades si se han inscrito oficialmente como persona jurídica y criminaliza las actividades que llevan a cabo grupos no inscritos[6].

E- No hay garantía de imparcialidad en el proceso de registro, debido a que el organismo de examen, Ministerio de Justicia, es dependiente del Gobierno. Los criterios de registro son lo suficientemente ambiguos para que las autoridades tengan amplias facultades discrecionales en su interpretación, lo que entraña denegaciones arbitrarias de registro de organizaciones de derechos humanos.

F- El gobierno toma medidas extremas y restrictivas para impedir el ejercicio del derecho de asociación, al no permitir la creación de nuevas organización alegando que ya existe una en ese mismo ámbito o asumen funciones estatales[7]. Ante la ausencia de respuesta o una decisión no justificada, no hay forma de interponer recurso de apelación.

[3] Los ciudadanos cubanos una vez cumplido los 14 años, o cuando inician en los diferentes niveles de educación (primario, básico, medio superior y Superior) son inscritos de oficio en las organizaciones sociales y de masa, como Comité de Defensa de la Revolución, Federación de Mujeres Cubanas (FMC), Organización de Pioneros José Martí", Federación de Estudiantes de la Enseñanza Media (FEEM), Federación de Estudiantes Universitarios (FEU), entre otras.

[4] Por ejemplo, a las entidades estatales empleadoras, los tribunales y órganos de investigación criminal solicitan a estas organizaciones que emitan criterios sobre la conducta individual del ciudadano, los cuales son tenidos en cuenta a la hora de otorgar un empleo o determinar la medida de la sanción a imponer en caso de comisión de un delito.

[5] Las asociaciones legalmente constituidas estas sometidas a un doble sistema de inspección que realizaran funcionarios del Departamento de Asociaciones del Ministerio de Justicia, para las asociaciones de carácter nacional, o de los registros provinciales, para las asociaciones provinciales y municipales. Por una parte. Después de constituida una asociación, esta debe firmar el documento contentivo de las normas de coordinación y colaboración con el órgano, organismo o dependencia estatal al que se presentara la solicitud. Estas normas Son de carácter permanente y supuestamente deben establecerse de común acuerdo teniendo en cuenta los objetivos que se propongan las actividades que se desarrollen y lo dispuesto en el reglamento. Una de ellas es la Realización de inspecciones periódicas a la asociación. Los órganos de relaciones realizan también inspecciones e informa a la oficina registral que corresponda de los resultados. Este doble sistema, garantiza que las decisiones que tomen los miembros o directiva de una organización se subordinen a lo que al respecto decida el departamento de asociación o el órgano de relación, so pena de poner en riesgo la existencia misma de la organización. Ambos órganos de control tiene la facultad, uno de proponer (órgano de relación), el otro de imponer (departamento de Asociaciones del Ministerio de Justicia) sanciones que pueden conducir a la disolución de la asociación.

[6] Artículo 208 de la Ley No. 62 de 29 de diciembre de 1987 "Código Penal. Esta ley considera un delito contra el orden público, las asociaciones ilícitas, entendida como aquellas organizaciones que no consten inscritas en el registro correspondiente, previendo para sus asociados o afiliados, sanción de privación de libertad de uno a tres meses o multa de hasta 5 mil pesos moneda nacional y para sus promotores o directores, sanción de privación de libertad de tres meses a un año o multa entre 100 y 15 mil pesos moneda nacional a trescientas cuotas

[7] la Dirección de Asociaciones del Ministerio de Justicia, al expedir su certificación, documento esencial para iniciar los trámites de legalización de una ONG que tengan por ejemplo fines educacionales advierte que los objetivos que se propone desarrollar en la pretendida asociación, son atribuciones y funciones que constitucionalmente conciernen al Estado y no se corresponde con los objetivos de una asociación

G- Las ideas que pueden "ofender, consternar o molestar"[8], son criminalizadas y las defensoras de los derechos humanos, a menudo son procesadas judicialmente, con el fin de disuadirlas de proseguir con sus actividades. Existen leyes que consideran toda declaración o actividad que cuestione las políticas gubernamentales dentro de la Isla, como subversiva y perturbadora del orden público, promovida y estimulada por el gobierno de Estados Unidos. Acciones tan sencillas como hablar vía telefónica, con una emisora de radio, opinar sobre políticas gubernamentales o participar en una manifestación pacífica, son causas suficientes para sufrir entre 2 y 15 años de prisión y/o multas entre 50 mil y 250 mil pesos[9].

Brigadas de Respuesta Rápida y los mítines de repudio

Individuos que defienden a ultranza el régimen político y sus dirigentes, actúan como parte de grupos, con la complicidad del Estado, se involucran cada vez más en los ataques contra defensoras. Estos actores no estatales amenazan, agreden y ofenden a las Damas de Blanco en un ambiente de impunidad, participan en manifestaciones violentas y se organizan en Brigadas de Respuesta Rápida (BRR), que se forman a nivel institucional, en centros laborales, estudio y barrio, a través de las organizaciones sociales y de masa.

El propio gobierno define y justifica las manifestaciones públicas de las BRR, como reacciones espontáneas del pueblo. En estos casos no tiene en cuenta las alteraciones del orden público[10]. Conocidas como "Mítines de Repudio" son utilizadas por las fuerzas de Seguridad nacional, para encubrir las detenciones violentas contra las Damas de Blanco. Las BRR, uniformados y agentes de la Seguridad del Estado actúan sincronizadamente y con total impunidad para impedir a las defensoras llegar a la misa y/o realizar la marcha pacífica.

Los manifestantes de las BRR se reúnen tanto en frente de la sede de las Damas de Blanco, como en las afueras de las iglesias católicas o de las viviendas particulares de las defensoras. También las interceptan en las calles por donde ellas transitan. Las autoridades le dan información del lugar, hora y día en que las defensoras realizarán sus actividades y también los lugares específicos donde deben interceptarlas o protagonizar el mitin de repudio.

---

[8] Delito de desacato
[9] Ley No. 88. Ley 88, Ley Mordaza, como se conoce en Cuba, tipifica y sanciona hechos, que según el gobierno cubano, están dirigidos a apoyar, facilitar o colaborar con los objetivos de la Ley "Helms -Burton", el bloqueo y la guerra económica, encaminados a quebrantar el orden interno, desestabilizar el país y liquidar el Estado Socialista y la independencia de Cuba. Las sanciones pueden duplicarse, si en los hechos participan, dos o más personas.
[10] La legislación penal cubana, sanciona al que provoque riñas o altercados en lugares al que concurren numerosas personas. La sanción se triplica si los actos hechos se realizan con el propósito de alterar de cualquier forma el orden público. Sin embargo los miembros de las BRR, actúan con total impunidad, porque los encargados de velar por la tranquilidad y seguridad ciudadana, los agentes policiales, no hacen absolutamente nada, cuando la propia ley les impone la obligación de actuar de oficio y detener al que intente cometer un delito, o en el momento de ir a cometerlo

CUBA SECTION OF TRAFFICKING IN PERSONS REPORT SUBMITTED BY THE HONORABLE CHRISTOPHER H. SMITH, A REPRESENTATIVE IN CONGRESS FROM THE STATE OF NEW JERSEY, AND CHAIRMAN, SUBCOMMITTEE ON AFRICA, GLOBAL HEALTH, GLOBAL HUMAN RIGHTS, AND INTERNATIONAL ORGANIZATIONS

and funded trafficking-related training for approximately 100 participants, including police officers, prosecutors, judges, social workers, labor inspectors, and diplomats preparing for assignments abroad. The training included two workshops for Croatian judges and prosecutors on secondary trauma of trafficking victims. The Croatian Border Police reported that 252 new Border Police Officers underwent three hours of trafficking-related training. The State Attorney's Office reported that up to 60 Croatian prosecutors attended Croatian government-funded trafficking-specific workshops and seminars in 2013 as either participants or lecturers. The government conducted cooperative international investigations with Bosnia and Herzegovina, Serbia, and Romania. The Government of Croatia did not report any investigations, prosecutions, or convictions of government employees complicit in human trafficking.

PROTECTION

The Croatian government sustained its victim protection efforts, but failed to screen vulnerable populations effectively for trafficking victims, particularly female minors who were victims of sex trafficking. The government funded three NGO-run trafficking shelters: one for adults, one for minors, and one alternate shelter that also houses victims of other forms of abuse. The government also provided three reception centers to provide victims with care before they could be transported to the shelters. Adult victims were allowed to leave shelters without chaperones after informing staff and completing a risk assessment. The Croatian government provided the equivalent of approximately $73,000 to fund the shelters in 2013, level with the amount it provided for shelter care in 2012. Foreign victims were offered the same standard of care as domestic victims, including shelter, medical care, education, legal assistance, psychological care, and assistance finding employment. The government's Office for Human Rights provided the equivalent of approximately $48,000 for victim assistance, professional training, and the anti-trafficking hotline.

Experts and government officials reported victim identification was inadequate in light of the suspected magnitude of the trafficking problem in Croatia. To remedy this, they suggested a comprehensive assessment of Croatia's trafficking problem. During the reporting period, the government identified 32 victims of trafficking, up from 13 victims identified during the previous reporting period; these figures included six women and 12 minor females who were sex trafficking victims; and nine adult males, four minor females, and one woman who were victims of forced labor, including forced begging. Government-funded NGOs offered care to 12 of these victims during the reporting period, with six of them receiving accommodation in shelters. At least some of the female minors were not initially identified as victims of trafficking and were released to their families without treatment or counselling.

The Ministry of Interior issued a standard operating procedure to guide police officers in identifying and transferring victims, which includes instructions on activating the national referral system when indicators of trafficking are present. Experts reported that the procedures themselves are effective, but that police officers, in particular, need to do a better job in identifying victims. According to the Ministry of Social Policy and Youth, there was a specially-designated social worker in each county responsible for providing initial victim care and coordinating further assistance. However, experts reported that the actual assistance provided in reintegrating trafficking victims was arranged on an *ad hoc* basis, and remained limited due to lack of funding.

Croatian law stipulates that foreign trafficking victims must not be deported, and are to be issued temporary residency permits for six months to one year, which can be periodically renewed based on subsequent needs assessments. Foreign victims also are entitled to employment assistance, skill development training, and adult classroom education. Alternatively, Croatian authorities and the Croatian Red Cross assist foreign trafficking victims with voluntary repatriation to their country of origin. The government encouraged victims to assist in investigating and prosecuting traffickers, but as a matter of policy did not force them to do so. Victims are entitled to assistance, including temporary residence permits for foreigners, regardless of whether they testify in trials. Victims also have the right to free legal representation, can file criminal charges and civil suits against their traffickers, and are entitled to seek financial compensation from the traffickers under a new law. Experts reported judges are sometimes overly aggressive when questioning trafficking victims on the witness stand, especially in cases where the victim has changed his or her story between talking to the police and testifying. Experts reported that trafficking victims were sometimes initially detained by police, but were usually released immediately upon being recognized as a trafficking victim. The State Attorney issued written instructions in June 2013 that victims must not be prosecuted for crimes committed as a result of being trafficked.

PREVENTION

The Croatian government continued efforts to prevent trafficking in persons, partnering with NGOs in the creation of a national action plan. The government continued to broadcast trafficking awareness public service announcements on public television. The Office for Human Rights and National Minorities also funded a new year-long public information campaign aimed at reducing the demand for women and girls trafficked for sexual exploitation, consisting of leaflets, billboards, and posters on public transportation, taxis, and bus and train stations, sensitizing potential customers to the reality that many persons engaged in prostitution may be trafficking victims. The Office for Human Rights also funded the development of new anti-trafficking pamphlets detailing indicators, prevention, and reporting guidance that are being distributed to border crossing checkpoints, illegal migrants, and asylum seekers. The government's efforts to reduce the demand for commercial sex continued to focus on Zagreb and the popular tourist destinations along the Adriatic coast, particularly during the summer tourism season. The government reported no prosecution of Croatian nationals traveling abroad for the purposes of international sex tourism during 2013. All Croatian diplomats and personnel deploying overseas undergo mandatory anti-trafficking training before they depart for their posting.

CUBA (Tier 3)

Cuba is a source country for adults and children subjected to sex trafficking, and possibly forced labor. Child prostitution and child sex tourism occur within Cuba. Cuban authorities report that young people from ages 13 to 20 are most vulnerable to human trafficking in Cuba. Cuban citizens have been subjected to forced prostitution outside of Cuba. There have been allegations of coerced labor with Cuban government work missions abroad; the Cuban government denies these allegations. Some Cubans participating in the work missions have stated that the postings are voluntary, and positions are well paid compared to jobs within Cuba. Others have claimed that Cuban authorities have coerced them, including by withholding their passports and restricting their movement. Some medical professionals participating in the missions have been able to take advantage of U.S. visas or immigration benefits, applying for those benefits and arriving in the United States in possession of their passports—an indication that at least some medical professionals retain possession of their passports. Reports of coercion by Cuban authorities in this program do not appear to reflect a uniform government policy of coercion; however, information is lacking. The government arranges for high school students in rural areas to harvest crops, but claims that this work is not coerced. The scope of trafficking involving Cuban citizens is difficult to verify because of sparse independent reporting, but in 2013 the Cuban government, for the first time, provided information to U.S. authorities regarding human trafficking in Cuba.

The Government of Cuba does not fully comply with the minimum standards for the elimination of trafficking and is not making significant efforts to do so. While the government has yet to establish a legal and policy framework prohibiting all forms of human trafficking and providing explicit victim protections, the government advised that it intends to amend its criminal code to ensure that it is in conformity with the requirements of the 2000 UN TIP Protocol, to which it acceded in July 2013. For the first time, the government released and reported concrete action against sex trafficking, including 10 prosecutions and corresponding convictions of sex traffickers in 2012 and the provision of services to the victims. Also, the Cuban government launched a media campaign to educate the Cuban public about trafficking and publicized its anti-trafficking services.

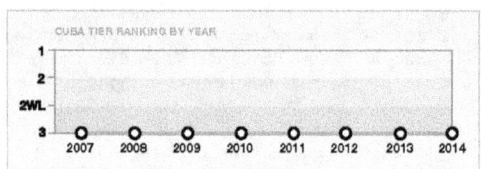

RECOMMENDATIONS FOR CUBA:
Revise existing anti-trafficking laws to incorporate a definition of trafficking that is consistent with the 2000 UN TIP Protocol; adopt a definition of a minor for the purposes of human trafficking consistent with the Protocol (under 18 years); continue and strengthen efforts, in partnership with international organizations, to provide specialized training for police, labor inspectors, social workers, and child protection specialists in identifying and protecting victims of sex trafficking and forced labor, including by having in place clear written policies and procedures to guide officials in the identification of trafficking victims, regardless of age or gender, and their referral to appropriate services; adopt policies that provide trafficking-specific, specialized assistance for male and female trafficking victims, including measures to ensure identified sex and labor trafficking victims are not punished for unlawful acts committed as a direct result of being subjected to sex trafficking or forced labor; enact and implement policies to ensure no use of coercion in Cuban work-abroad missions; provide specialized training for managers of work-abroad missions in identifying and protecting victims of forced labor; criminally prosecute both sex trafficking and forced labor; and continue funding and expand the victim-centered practices of three government

facilities for collection of testimony of young children.

PROSECUTION
The Government of Cuba prosecuted and convicted sex trafficking cases, but its overall effort was hampered by the absence of a comprehensive legal framework that criminalizes all forms of human trafficking. Cuba prohibits some forms of human trafficking through the following laws: Article 299.1 (pederasty with violence); Article 300.1 (lascivious abuse); Article 302 (procuring and trafficking in persons); Article 303 (sexual assault); Article 310.1 (corruption of minors for sexual purposes); Article 312.1 (corruption of minors for begging); and Article 316.1 (sale and trafficking of a child under 16). The Cuban penal code's definition of sex trafficking appears to conflate sex trafficking with prostitution and pimping. The law criminalizes adult sex trafficking achieved through force, coercion, or abuse of power or a position of vulnerability, although the use of such means is considered an aggravating factor (to a crime of inducing or benefitting from prostitution), not an integral part of the crime. It does not explicitly include the use of fraud and physical force within the list of aggravating factors that make coercion of prostitution a crime. The provision addressing corruption of minors encompasses many of the forms of child sex trafficking, but its definition of a minor as a child under 16 years old is inconsistent with the definition under the 2000 UN TIP Protocol, which defines a child as any person under the age of 18; this means 16- and 17-year-olds engaged in prostitution for the benefit of a third party would not necessarily be identified as trafficking victims. Although anyone inducing children between the ages of 16 and 18 to engage in prostitution would not be identified as traffickers under Cuban law, forced prostitution is illegal irrespective of age of the victim, and the government has prosecuted individuals benefitting from the prostitution of children. Victims under 18 were clearly identified by the Cuban government in 2012 as trafficking victims, and the perpetrators of these crimes were punished more severely in some cases when the victim was younger than 16. Both adult and child sex trafficking provisions fail explicitly to criminalize recruitment, transport, and receipt of persons for these purposes. Cuba became a party to the 2000 UN TIP Protocol during the reporting period and has indicated that it is engaged in the process of generally revising its criminal code, including so that it will meet its obligations as a State Party.

In a positive step toward greater transparency, in 2013, the government presented official data on investigations and prosecutions of sex trafficking offenses and convictions of sex trafficking offenders. In 2012, the year covered by the most recent official Cuban report, the government reported 10 prosecutions and corresponding convictions of sex traffickers. At least six of the convictions involved nine child sex trafficking victims within Cuba, including the facilitation of child sex tourism in Cuba. The average sentence was nine years' imprisonment. The government reported that a government employee (a teacher) was investigated, prosecuted, and convicted of a sex trafficking offense. There were no reported forced labor prosecutions or convictions. Child protection specialists reportedly provided training to police academy students. Students at the Ministry of Interior academy and police who were assigned to tourist centers reportedly received specific anti-trafficking training. The government reported that employees of the Ministries of Tourism and Education received training to spot indicators of trafficking, particularly among children engaged in commercial sex. The government demonstrated its willingness to cooperate with other governments on investigations of possible traffickers.

PROTECTION

The government made efforts to protect victims during the reporting period. Authorities reported that they identified nine child sex trafficking victims and four adult sex trafficking victims linked to the 2012 convictions; authorities reported no identified labor trafficking victims or male victims. Though the government had systems in place to identify and assist a broader group of vulnerable women and children, including trafficking victims, the government did not share any documentation of trafficking-specific procedures to guide officials in proactively identifying trafficking victims among vulnerable groups and referring them to available services. For example, the Federation of Cuban Women, a government entity that also receives funding from international organizations, operates 173 Guidance Centers for Women and Families nationwide and reported that these centers provided assistance to 2,480 women and families harmed by violence, including victims of trafficking. These centers assisted the women from their initial contact with law enforcement through prosecution of the offenders. Social workers at the Guidance Centers provided services for victims of trafficking and other crimes such as psychological treatment, health care, skills training, and assistance in finding employment. The four adult trafficking victims identified by the Cuban government reportedly received services at these Guidance Centers. Authorities reported that the Ministry of Education identified other sex trafficking cases while addressing school truancy incidents. The government did not operate any shelters or services specifically for adult trafficking victims.

The police encouraged child trafficking victims under the age of 17 to assist in prosecutions of traffickers by operating three facilities where law enforcement and social workers worked together to support the collection of testimony and the treatment of sexually and physically abused children. These victim-centered facilities gathered children's testimony though psychologist led videotaped interviewing, usually removing the need for children to appear in court. In addition to collecting testimony, government social workers developed a specific plan for the provision of follow-on services. The facilities assisted the nine identified child trafficking victims and reportedly referred them to longer term psychological care, shelter, and other services as needed.

The government asserted that none of the identified victims were punished, and authorities reported having policies that ensured identified victims were not punished for crimes committed as a direct result of being subjected to human trafficking. There were no reports of foreign trafficking victims in Cuba.

PREVENTION

The government reported on its anti-trafficking prevention efforts. During the year, state media produced newspaper articles and television and radio programs to raise public awareness about trafficking. Senior public officials, including the Minister of Justice, publicly raised the problem of trafficking. The government maintained an Office of Security and Protection within the Ministry of Tourism charged with monitoring Cuba's image as a tourism destination and combating sex tourism. The government did not report the existence of an established anti-trafficking taskforce or structured monitoring mechanism.

A formal, written report on the government's anti-trafficking efforts was released to the public in October 2013.

CURACAO (Tier 2)*

Curacao is a source, transit, and destination country for women, children, and men who are subjected to sex trafficking and forced labor. Police arrested a suspected Colombian trafficker in Curacao in April 2013; authorities indicated the suspect used debt bondage, withheld sex trafficking victims' personal documents, held them against their will, and subjected them to physical and psychological abuse in public establishments in Curacao. It is unclear how the recruitment process works for Curacao's walled, legal brothel that offers "24/7 access to more than 120" foreign women in prostitution. Local authorities believe that migrant workers have been subjected to forced domestic service and forced labor in construction, landscaping, and retail. Some migrants in restaurants and local businesses are vulnerable to debt bondage. Officials reported undocumented Cuban nationals were vulnerable to trafficking in Curacao given their lack of travel documents and inability to work legally in the country. Authorities also reported Indian and Chinese nationals remained vulnerable to forced labor in the country. Foreign trafficking victims originate predominantly from Colombia, the Dominican Republic, Haiti, and Asia. Organizations in Venezuela have also reported assisting trafficking victims who were exploited in Curacao. A 2013 UN Report on Curacao cited a UN Committee recommendation to strengthen its efforts to address child sexual exploitation and trafficking.

The Government of Curacao does not fully comply with the minimum standards for the elimination of trafficking; however, it is making significant efforts to do so. During the year, the government initiated new trafficking investigations, continued to investigate a high-profile sex trafficking case involving a police officer, and established a multi-disciplinary anti-trafficking taskforce. However, it did not identify any trafficking victims nor convict any traffickers in 2013. The lack of standard operating procedures on victim identification for all front-line responders, including immigration officers and health workers, hindered the government's ability to identify trafficking victims and increased the risk of victims' inadvertent arrest and deportation.

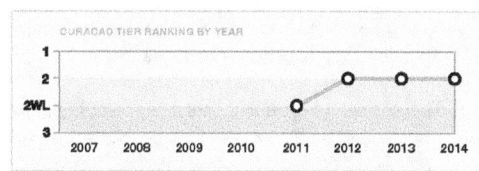

RECOMMENDATIONS FOR CURACAO:

Make a robust and transparent effort to identify and assist potential victims of sex trafficking and forced labor by implementing formal proactive victim protection measures to guide officials, including health workers, on how to identify victims and how to assist victims of forced labor and sex trafficking in the legal and illegal sex trade; vigorously prosecute trafficking offenses and convict and punish trafficking offenders, including any

* Curacao is a semi-autonomous entity within the Kingdom of the Netherlands. The Kingdom Charter divides responsibility among the co-equal parts of the Kingdom based on jurisdiction. For the purpose of this report, Curacao is not a "country" to which the minimum standards for the elimination of trafficking in the Trafficking Victims Protection Act apply. This narrative reflects how Curacao would be assessed if it were a separate, independent country.

LETTER TO PRESIDENT OBAMA FROM THE STFA SUBMITTED BY THE HONORABLE CHRISTOPHER H. SMITH, A REPRESENTATIVE IN CONGRESS FROM THE STATE OF NEW JERSEY, AND CHAIRMAN, SUBCOMMITTEE ON AFRICA, GLOBAL HEALTH, GLOBAL HUMAN RIGHTS, AND INTERNATIONAL ORGANIZATIONS

State Troopers' Fraternal Association of New Jersey, Inc.

MICHAEL P. ZANYOR
1ˢᵗ VICE PRESIDENT

DANIEL M. OLIVEIRA
2ᴺᴰ VICE PRESIDENT

WAYNE D. BLANCHARD
VICE PRESIDENT FOR LEGISLATION
AND GRIEVANCES

JAMES E. NUZZI
TREASURER

WILLIAM D. LEGG
SECRETARY FOR RESOLUTIONS

CHRISTOPHER J. BURGOS
PRESIDENT

STEVEN KUHN
CORRESPONDING SECRETARY

CHARLES LEWANDOWSKI
RECORDING SECRETARY

RICHARD MONDRAGON
SERGEANT-AT-ARMS

ROBERT H. PAVELCHAK
SERGEANT-AT-ARMS

RICHARD D. LOCCKE
ASSOCIATION COUNSEL

December 22, 2014

The Honorable Barack Obama
President of the United States
The White House
Washington, D.C. 20500

Dear President Obama:

We at the State Troopers Fraternal Association of New Jersey represent the interests of approximately 8,000 NJ Troopers since our founding in 1921, which includes active, retired, deceased, and the Sixty-Seven NJ State Troopers who paid the ultimate price of being killed in the line of duty.

There is no doubt that the Castro regime has a long history of repression, despotism and brutality that has forced countless Cubans to seek refuge in the U.S. in search of a better life. We do not share your view that restoring diplomatic relations without a clear commitment from the Cuban government of the steps they will take to reverse decades of human rights violations will result in a better and more just Cuba for its people. However, despite our profound disagreement with this decision, we believe there is an opportunity for Cuba and its government to show the American people and the citizens of the State of New Jersey, it is serious about change.

The Cuban government has been providing safe haven to convicted murderer Joanne Chesimard, a woman designated by the Federal Bureau of Investigation as a domestic terrorist, and the first woman ever placed on the FBI's Most Wanted Terrorist List.

In New Jersey, Joanne Chesimard is notorious for her role in the cold-blooded execution-style killing of New Jersey State Trooper Werner Foerster, Badge #2608, and seriously wounding New Jersey State Trooper James Harper, Badge #2108. On May 2, 1973, Chesimard, Clark Squire and Zayd Shakur were pulled over on the New Jersey Turnpike by Troopers Foerster and Harper for a motor vehicle violation. Chesimard and both men in the car were armed with semi-automatic handguns, and possessed fictitious identification. During the motor vehicle stop, Chesimard initiated a gun battle, wounding Trooper Harper. In the shootout that followed, Chesimard's weapon was used to shoot Trooper Foerster in the abdomen and then, as he lay incapacitated on the ground, Trooper Foerster's own weapon was used against him and he was brutally executed with two bullets to the head.

Chesimard was convicted in 1977 of first-degree murder and a number of other charges stemming from this horrific incident and sentenced to life in prison. Chesimard, aided and abetted by armed accomplices, escaped from a NJ prison in 1979 and has been a fugitive from justice ever since. It is believed that she moved to Cuba in 1984 and has, since that time, lived freely there, attending government functions and being provided with housing, food, transportation and security by the Cuban government.

A long history of bipartisan support exists for the need to bring this convicted murderer back to the United States so she can be made to serve the prison time she was sentenced to more than thirty-seven years ago. A few important points to consider:

- In 1998, the US. House of Representatives passed Concurrent Resolution 254 by a vote of 371-0 requesting that the Cuban government return Chesimard to the United States;

- In 1998, the US. Senate passed Concurrent Resolution 254 by unanimous consent requesting that the Cuban government return Chesimard to the United States;

- In 2005, the Department of Justice approved an increase in the reward for Chesimard's capture to $1 million; and

- In 2013, the Federal Bureau of Investigation placed Chesimard on its Most Wanted Terrorist List, designated her as a "domestic terrorist" and increased the reward for her capture to $2 million.

Cuba's provision of safe harbor to Chesimard by providing political asylum to a convicted cop killer, and her ability to elude justice, is an affront to every resident of our state, our country, and in particular, the men and women of the New Jersey State Police, who have tirelessly tried to bring this killer back to justice.

We urge you to demand the immediate return of Chesimard before any further consideration of restoration of diplomatic relations with the Cuban government. In addition, there certainly can be no review of Cuba's designation as a State Sponsor of Terrorism until Joanne Chesimard, a person designated by the FBI as a domestic terrorist, is returned to the United States.

If, as you assert, Cuba is serious about embracing democratic principles then this action would be an essential first step. We ask you to use this opportunity to engage with the Cuban government to get this resolved, as we are very disappointed that returning a convicted killer of a State Trooper was not already demanded and accomplished in the context of the steps you announced regarding this despotic dictatorship.

The family of her victims, like so many of those who have, and continue to suffer under the Castro regime, deserve this basic human decency before further steps towards Cuba are taken by the U.S.

Sincerely,

Christopher J. Burgos, President
New Jersey State Troopers Fraternal Association
President@stfa.org
www.stfa.org

Statement by Rep. Chris Smith on Respecting the Human Rights of All While Combatting Boko Haram In Nigeria.

All governments have a duty to protect everyone and I am unequivocally opposed to acts of violence against anyone.

All individuals, including LGBT persons, should be treated with respect and compassion.

Regrettably, recent political attacks have attempted to distort my position and extensive record defending human rights.

At a recent House Foreign Affairs Subcommittee on Africa and Human Rights hearing on combating violence inflicted by the terrorist group Boko Haram in Nigeria—the fourth such hearing on the topic I have convened in the past three years alone—I asked the Obama Administration witness, Principal Deputy Assistant Secretary Robert T. Jackson, Bureau of African Affairs, U.S. Department of State, two questions.

First, I inquired if the administration's view on LGBT, which differs from the Nigerian position, "affected in any way or in any way hindered U.S. support to Nigeria to combat Boko Haram?" Second, I asked, "... has the administration held back or in any way affected funding to the faith community, whether it be Muslim or Christian, in the dissemination of those funds to combat malaria or any of the other problems faced by Nigerians?", including assisting Internally Displaced Persons.

Mr. Jackson replied "there had been no impact."

My interactions with African officials and religious leaders led to my questions about US policy in Nigeria. This is a war-torn country where the most horrific violence is perpetrated by terrorist groups, most notably Boko Haram. U.S. humanitarian assistance is needed and sought not just by the government but by NGOs—including faith-based NGOs which often have the aid infrastructures and the trust of the people but which do not always agree with the policies of the U.S. administration.

I also noted at the hearing that there are "fundamental differences in the United States over the whole LGBT issue" and that I am a "strong believer in traditional marriage" and do not "construe homosexual rights as human rights" while acknowledging that "others have a different view and I certainly respect them."

There is no consensus in the U.S. or globally supporting homosexual marriage as a human right.

My record is consistent in demonstrating support for democratic rule and universally recognized human rights for all. It is unfortunate that political foes are using the volatile situation in Nigeria to distort my record and push their own political interests.

Over the years I have built a record advancing the protection of all human life and opposing acts of violence. I have fought on behalf of abused and/or disenfranchised people in the U.S., China, Vietnam, Russia, eastern Europe, Northern Ireland, and throughout Africa—including signing a congressional letter to Ugandan President Museveni opposing legislation that would penalize a single act of homosexual conduct with a life sentence and a mandatory death penalty if the person is HIV-positive.